AT HOME

WITH

Simon Wood

FINE DINING MADE SIMPLE
FROM THE MASTERCHEF CHAMPION 2015

Acknowledgements

For their love, support, encouragement and honesty; thank you to my nearest and dearest, my new second home (OAFC) and my loyal and supportive team.

For all the amazing suppliers of ingredients, goods and equipment I thank you – you give me the tools to work with.

And to MasterChef and John and Gregg for believing in me and setting me on this exciting road and unbelievable experience.

Finally a thank you to my publishers, Meze Publishing, for their hard work and belief in my vision.

This is just the beginning.

Thank You

AT HOME WITH SIMON WOOD: FINE DINING MADE SIMPLE

©2016 Meze Publishing

First edition printed in 2016 in the UK.

ISBN: 978-1-910863-11-4

Written by: Simon Wood and Rachel Heward

Edited by: Phil Turner

Photography by: Marc Barker

Additional Photography: Tom Astley

Cover photo shot at Russell Hutton, Sheffield

Designed by: Paul Cocker

PR: Plank PR

Contributors: Stephen Coyne, Emily Beaumont

Published by Meze Publishing Limited
Unit 1 Beehive Works
Milton Street
Sheffield S3 7WL
Web: www.mezepublishing.co.uk
Tel: 0114 275 7709
Email: info@mezepublishing.co.uk

Printed by Bell and Bain Ltd, Glasgow

Contents

Becoming a MasterChef

How it all began

My first food memory takes me back to my grandmother's kitchen at the weekend. I'd watch eagerly as she bustled around baking and cooking for the extended family, giving me the privilege of the first taste test whilst she worked. Looking back now it was really just traditional northern cooking, but as a wide-eyed child things like rabbit always appeared infinitely more adventurous than what we'd have at home.

> **I'd spend most of my day preoccupied with what I was going to cook for dinner. I'd be sat at my desk and although my day revolved around numbers and spreadsheets, food was always at the forefront of my mind.**

Since then I've always tried to recreate that sense of adventure in the kitchen, so my approach to home cooking would push the boundaries of your average meat-and-two-veg dinner. At first cooking my evening meal was just a way to relax and unwind, but then it became an obsession of sorts. I'd spend most of my day preoccupied with what I was going to cook for dinner. I'd be sat at my desk and although my day revolved around numbers and spreadsheets, food was always at the forefront of my mind. I craved the creativity that coming up with new ideas and concepts for dishes gave me.

You can learn from everywhere and anywhere. I'd pour through piles of cookery books, watch videos and tutorials online, and get inspiration from dining out. I'd advocate any method of learning, you'll get there as long as you apply yourself, take your time, be patient – and be prepared to eat a disaster or two along the way! It's all about pushing yourself to do something you've never done before, and finding the fun in the experimentation of it all.

The big break

I watched MasterChef from day one and always wanted to put myself up for it, but wasn't quite brave enough until last year. I took the plunge and managed to get on the first time I applied, though it wasn't an easy process. You have to battle through an online application and two telephone interviews before you're even allowed near a stove, and then you have to impress the producers with a signature dish. Finally, I found myself in the MasterChef kitchen amongst the top forty, not quite believing my luck.

It was my chance to wow the judges. I always knew what I would do at this stage, and I stuck to my guns by serving up a simple but effective chicken and chorizo tortellini. After perfecting the pasta (which I had practised countless times) there's really not much that can go wrong with a classic flavour combination like that. It won dish of the day and I got straight through.

> **Finally, I found myself in the MasterChef kitchen amongst the top forty, not quite believing my luck ... It was my chance to wow the judges.**

MasterChef was the opportunity of a lifetime, not to mention a huge learning curve. Without it I'd never have had the chance work alongside some of the best in the business, including the likes of Michelin-starred Michael Caines, three-starred chef Massimo Bottura and the legend Marcus Wareing – not to mention John and Gregg themselves. Working at Simon Rimmer's restaurant Greens in particular inspired me to broaden my horizons when it comes to vegetarian food.

But it wasn't all plain-sailing. One of the hardest parts of the show was how the filming of it interfered with making the dish itself. Now that may sound strange but it's more difficult than you think to talk to the cameras whilst cooking, especially as your time doesn't stop during that point. It really pushes your multitasking skills to the limit!

Because of MasterChef I have learnt to take criticism, move on and evolve from it. It's one of the best ways to learn from mistakes and advance to the next level. However, you can't forget that food is subjective, so it's important to trust your instincts and not let what other people think completely change your style.

Dream job

After winning MasterChef I had to keep quiet for three months before it was aired. I wasn't allowed to utter a word of the outcome to my friends, family or anyone. This huge thing had just happened in my life and I had to go back to my day job – it was excruciating! But I sat tight, and I've been rewarded tenfold. I have always wanted a job where I could cook all day, use my passion and be creative. Until now I never had the platform to do this unless I wanted to start from the bottom, which is difficult to do when you're trying to raise a family. MasterChef has given me the opportunity to skip all of that and jump right into a position where I can play around with whole menus and cook for hundreds of people. What makes this even more special is that it all happens under the roof of my boyhood football team, Oldham Athletic.

I change the menu weekly for match days, depending upon the produce available. I try to source everything as locally as possible, and I take more influence from seasonal produce and getting the most out of each ingredient, rather than sticking to a particular style of cooking like French or Italian. It's all about enhancing classic combinations and playing around with flavours that complement each other. I find sticking to a certain set of "rules" restricting, which is why the food I cook incorporates many styles, cuisines and cultures.

> **What makes this even more special is that it all happens under the roof of my boyhood football team Oldham Athletic.**

The private dining events that we offer at Oldham have become extremely popular, as we aim to serve up something people can't make at home; food that provides that wow factor. After all, that's what you go out for. This book, however, will be giving you an insight into how to do that for yourself. With these recipes, tips and tricks, I'm hoping to show you how to enhance your meals, so you'll be cooking up restaurant quality food in your own kitchen.

Using this book

My ethos is simple: food that tastes great and looks good in equal measure. It's about the whole experience. When you're about to eat a meal you make a judgement in your head based on how it looks without having even tried it. It's like judging a book by its cover, but for food. For that reason I've always been interested in and passionate about the way my meals look. The idea is that it's perfect from start to finish.

For this, attention to detail is key; all it takes is patience and a tiny bit of effort. For example you can take the classic British favourite of steak and chips and elevate it to look extraordinary by slicing the steak differently, shaping the potatoes more delicately, taking care with the plating and thinking outside the box when it comes to garnishes. You'll notice I often don't overload the plate with ingredients to ensure the dish looks stunning when it lands on the table. You can always put a dish of extras in the middle for your guests to share once they've cleaned their plate.

> **My ethos is simple: food that tastes great and looks good in equal measure.**

To help you along your way, I've dedicated a whole section to the art of plating up, and another chapter provides staple recipes that are extremely simple, but add that extra element to take the dish to the next level. I've done my best to cover all bases and have broken the book down into sections that include everything from meat dishes to seafood, pasta, salads, vegetarian, dessert and a good selection of non-gluten dishes too.

Whilst some of the recipes may appear a bit complicated or daunting, my advice to you is this: take your time and as much care with each element as you did with the last, and go that extra mile when it comes to picking ingredients and serving up. The recipes here are representative of the journey I've been on, from an (albeit obsessive) home cook to professional chef. I came up with the majority of them in my own kitchen, so they're designed perfectly for yours.

The core of this book is fine dining made simple. Whilst we all love going out, I've always found that it is immensely more satisfying to create a visually stunning and delicious dish for yourself, so this is what I'd like to share with you. Go on, give it a go!

Super Salads

Tomato and mozzarella with basil oil and basil and chorizo crisps

Serves 4

This is a simple dish, one you can prepare in advance and serve at room temperature – you should never serve tomatoes straight from the fridge anyway as they have far more flavour at room temperature. Because of the simple preparation, you'll have time to put extra effort into the presentation, taking extra care to make sure everything is uniform on the plate.

INGREDIENTS

75g mozzarella per person

12 ripe plum tomatoes

Sliced chorizo or my chorizo crumb

150ml olive oil, plus extra for frying

Fresh basil

Sea salt and white pepper

Micro basil

Belazu balsamic vinegar

For the chorizo crumb

Chorizo

Olive Oil

METHOD

Drain the mozzarella and slice evenly into 1cm thick rounds. Use your smallest round cutter to make tiny circles of cheese, and season to taste.

Have a bowl of boiling water ready. Using a sharp knife make a small cross in the bottom of the tomatoes, drop into the hot water for 20 seconds then remove. The skins should now slide off easily. Quarter the tomatoes and remove the seeds. Using the same cutter as before, make little rounds of tomato.

You can use the chorizo crumb recipe below but sometimes, for this dish, I like to make something that is a little different.

Take some sliced chorizo and roll it into a tube. Pierce with a fork and then carefully hold it in some hot oil to evenly crisp up the chorizo tube.

Arrange the tomato, mozzarella and chorizo on the plate like in the photo.

For the dressing put the olive oil and basil in a food processor and season well. Mix together thoroughly and drizzle over the dish. Finish with the micro basil leaves and a little balsamic vinegar.

For the chorizo crumb

This is so simple to make that you can afford to spend a little time on the prep. I prefer the chorizo to be cut uniformly into dice of around 5mm square – the devil is in the detail and little accurate touches like this will give the dish that wow factor!

Once you have diced your chorizo simply add a tablespoon of olive oil into a large cold frying pan followed by your chorizo. I use a cold pan as this allows the oil in the chorizo to warm through gently and render down into that lovely dressing for your dish.

Once the chorizo is brown and crispy, drain onto some kitchen paper and store the oil in a jar to use later.

Curry spiced new potato and turmeric egg salad

Serves 4

Turn a classic potato and egg salad into something more elegant by taking time to source more interesting ingredients like these salad blue potatoes. To take it further, experiment by using different sized cutters to shape the potatoes and take your time when plating.

INGREDIENTS

600g salad blue potatoes, (if you cannot get these use a nice Charlotte or Anya variety)

1 tsp chilli powder

3 tsp turmeric powder

1 white onion, quartered

½ tsp mustard seeds

1 tsp white pepper

2 curry leaves

1 bay leaf

3 cloves garlic

4 free range eggs

50g butter

Sea salt and white pepper

Fresh coriander

Baby watercress

Turmeric to garnish

METHOD

Chop the potatoes into bite-sized pieces. Fill a large saucepan with water leaving enough room for the potatoes, and add the chilli and turmeric powder. Next add the onion, mustard seeds, white pepper, curry and bay leaves. Add the garlic and season well. Add the potatoes and then bring to the boil until they have softened.

Take the deepest saucepan you have and bring the water to just under a boil. Crack the egg into a cup first and then when the water is at the right temperature gently pour it in. Cook for 2½ minutes and then remove from the water with a slotted spoon.

Take a clove of garlic out of the potatoes and use the back of a knife to crush it into a paste. Gently melt the butter then add the garlic and season well.

When plating, you can use a chef ring in the centre of a plate and stack up the potatoes, taking care not to add any of the aromatics in the water, or scatter stylishly as I have here.

Add the whole egg onto the top of the stack of potatoes and then halve it so you don't lose any yolk. Top with coriander and watercress and then drizzle over a tablespoon of the melted garlic butter. Scatter a little turmeric and you're ready to go.

Crispy lamb salad
with baba ganoush and flatbread

Serves 4

This dish was inspired by a lamb kebab but I have stripped it back to make it more delicate, deconstructing it on the plate so you can see each delicious element.

INGREDIENTS

For the crispy lamb

2kg lamb shoulder on the bone

300ml red wine

150ml water

2 lemons, halved

2 red onions, halved

1 bulb garlic, halved

For the flat bread

300g self-raising flour

1 tsp baking powder

300g natural yoghurt

½ tsp sea salt

1 tsp black onion seeds

For the garnish

Bunch fresh coriander

1 pomegranate

For the baba ganoush

1 whole bulb garlic

3 large aubergines

½ lemon, juiced

3 tbsp tahini paste

1 pinch ground cumin

3 tbsp extra virgin olive oil

Sea salt and white pepper, to taste

1 pinch smoked paprika

1 tbsp fresh flat-leaf parsley, chopped

METHOD

Preheat the oven to 160°c. In a large frying pan seal the lamb and then place it onto a wire rack on a roasting tray. Add the wine, water, lemons, onions and garlic into the bottom of the tray.

Cover with foil to prevent any moisture escaping. Place in the oven to cook slowly for 4 hours. Remember to check that the liquid hasn't evaporated; you can add some more stock or water if it looks low.

When the lamb is ready leave it to rest for 30 minutes before pulling into rustic chunks.

For the flat bread

Simply mix all of the flat bread ingredients together in a bowl, cover with cling film and set aside to rest for 20 minutes.

Once rested use lightly floured hands to roll into evenly sized balls. Flatten and then toast in a dry frying pan until golden on both sides.

Remove the onions from the roasting tray, drain and slice thinly. Next halve the pomegranate and use the back of a tablespoon to remove the seeds from inside. Delicately place the lamb around the arc of a clean plate. Use a cutter to shape the flatbread and carefully garnish with onion, coriander and pomegranate seeds, not forgetting the amazingly flavoursome baba ganoush.

For the baba ganoush

Preheat your oven to 170°c and slow roast the garlic until softened.

Prick the aubergines with a fork and place under a hot grill until the skin is charred and blackened. Then place in the oven at 170°c for 15 minutes, or until the flesh feels soft when you press it.

In a pestle and mortar, crush 3 cloves of the sweet roasted garlic with the lemon juice, tahini, cumin, olive oil and salt and pepper.

When cool enough to handle, cut the aubergines in half and scoop out the flesh. Add the softened part of the warm aubergines into the pestle and mortar with the remaining ingredients.

Place in a serving dish and finish with a drizzle of olive oil and sprinkle the paprika and parsley over the top, before finishing with a drizzle of olive oil.

Courgette ribbons with pesto and charred cherry tomatoes

Serves 4

This is a really simple salad that is packed with flavour. It also serves as a nice gluten free alternative to pasta.

INGREDIENTS

For the roasted cherry tomatoes

6 cherry tomatoes per person, halved

1 tbsp pesto

1 tbsp olive oil

Sea salt

For the courgette ribbons

4 medium to large courgettes

1 tbsp olive oil

1½ tbsp pesto per person

Fresh parsley, chopped

A few carefully selected small basil leaves

For the pesto

50g pine nuts

2 cloves garlic

Pinch sea salt

Two large bunches basil

50g Parmesan

150ml olive oil

½ lemon, juiced

METHOD

For the pesto

In a large frying pan toast the pine nuts until golden.

Next use the back of your knife to crush the garlic into a smooth paste. A little sea salt will help to do this.

I make my pesto in a food processor, but you can use a pestle and mortar. With the exception of the lemon juice add in all the remaining ingredients and blitz into a smooth paste. Taste and add the lemon juice and adjust the seasoning accordingly.

This will go amazingly well with pasta, meat or roasted vegetables.

For the roasted cherry tomatoes

Halve the tomatoes and place in a bowl with the basil pesto and coat evenly. Add the olive oil and season with sea salt. Roast cut side down in an oven at 200°c for five minutes, or pop them into a dry frying pan until charred.

For the courgette ribbons

Halve the courgettes lengthways. Using a speed peeler in one long motion simply peel away making ribbons. You can use a mandoline if you prefer, but this is the safest way to do it.

Take a large frying pan and add in the olive oil, followed by the courgettes. They only need a minute or two to warm through and are delicious hot or cold. Next add in the pesto and parsley and stir until the courgettes are evenly coated.

Use a pair of tongues, serve into a warm bowl, and top with your roasted cherry tomatoes and basil leaves.

Fennel with sweet caramelised chicory and orange salad

Serves 4

This dish is very light, perfect for a dinner party starter. The aniseed flavour from the fennel is complemented wonderfully by the juicy orange pieces and bittersweet caramelised chicory.

INGREDIENTS

75g fennel per person

Olive oil

Sea salt and white pepper

1 lemon, juiced

Fresh tarragon

2 oranges, one segmented with the pith removed

30ml olive oil

½ orange, juiced

½ chicory per person

For the caramelised chicory

2 white chicories

Caster sugar

Olive oil

25g butter

METHOD

Preheat your oven to 190°c.

Remove the delicate fronds from the top of the fennel and save for the garnish later. Slice the fennel into four pieces and toss in olive oil, sea salt and white pepper. Roast until softened then set aside in a bowl and dress in lemon juice and finely chopped tarragon.

To add that extra punch of flavour as well as a stunning visual element, take a blow torch and on a metal tray (not your kitchen work surface!) blacken one side of the orange segments.

Delicately dress your plate with all of the elements, keeping the ingredients tightly together in the middle of it.

For the dressing, mix together the olive oil and orange juice and season well. Mix again thoroughly and drizzle over the dish.

Add the fennel fronds on top to serve.

For the caramelised chicory

Remove any damaged outer leaves and cut in half lengthways.

Heat a small amount of olive oil in a hot frying pan. Sprinkle a little caster sugar over the cut surface of the chicories and place in the hot frying pan, cut-side down. Cover with greaseproof paper and when the surface is golden add in a knob of butter and baste over the top of the chicory until evenly coated and softened.

Spinach falafel with spiced yoghurt and leaves

Serves 4

You can shape this falafel in a mould like I've done or you can go for the more traditional spherical shape. Either way it packs a huge amount of flavour, especially when combined with the delicately spiced yoghurt.

INGREDIENTS

For the falafel

720g cooked chickpeas

2 red onions, chopped

4 cloves garlic, crushed into a paste

1 bag spinach

4 tbsp fresh parsley

½ tsp ground cumin

½ tsp ground coriander

1 tsp sea salt

½ tsp white pepper

1 lemon, juice and zest

75g plain flour, plus extra for dusting

½ tsp baking powder

2 tbsp breadcrumbs

Oil, for frying

For the spiced yoghurt

½ tsp powdered ginger

½ tsp ground turmeric

1 tsp cayenne pepper

250g Greek yoghurt, I like to use Total 0%

Chilli oil

For garnish

Mixed salad leaves

METHOD

For the falafel

Making the falafel is really quick and super simple, just add all of the ingredients into a food processor and blitz into a smooth paste. Leave to chill in the fridge for 30 minutes before using wet hands to roll them into even sized spheres or shape into rectangular moulds. It is important you keep the size the same to ensure even cooking. If you really want to impress you could weigh the mixture to make sure they are the same, around 8g is about right.

To cook the falafel simply drop into hot oil at 190°c until golden and crisp, around 3-4 minutes.

For the spiced yoghurt

Combine all the spiced yoghurt ingredients and serve with a drizzle of chilli oil and a fresh leaf salad.

Shredded beef and rocket with a horseradish cream and caramelised shallots

Serves 4

My spicy horseradish cream is the perfect accompaniment to this slow cooked beef brisket, along with a handful of peppery rocket. A salad for those who don't like salads!

INGREDIENTS

For the beef
2kg beef brisket
500ml beef stock

For the horseradish cream
50g fresh horseradish root
3g salt
350ml double cream
0.3g xanthan gum (this is easily bought online)

To serve
2 shallots per person
Rocket leaves

For the Melba toasts (optional)
White bread

METHOD

For the beef
Preheat the oven to 160°c.

In a large frying pan seal the brisket and then place it on to a wire rack on a roasting tray, adding the beef stock into the bottom of the tray.

Cover with foil to prevent any moisture escaping. Place in the oven to cook slowly for 5 hours. Remember to check that the liquid hasn't evaporated; you can add some more stock or water if it looks low.

For the horseradish cream
Peel and grate the horseradish root and combine with the salt, cream and xanthan gum. Refrigerate until the beef is ready. The longer you leave it, the more intense the flavour will be; I like it really hot!

When the beef is ready, leave it to rest for 30 minutes before shredding with two forks.

While the beef is resting strain the cream through a sieve and then whip gently in a clean bowl. Add it to a squeezy bottle ready to serve.

Take the juices from the bottom of the roasting tray and reduce by half in a saucepan. Then pour them back over the shredded beef, ready to serve.

I use a 4cm square chef ring to plate this dish and allow 3 squares per person. Press the beef into the mould to hold its shape and then add the rocket, caramelised shallots (see page 177) and dots of the horseradish cream.

For the Melba toasts
These are simple to make and with a little extra effort can look visually stunning on this dish.

Take a rolling pin and some white bread with the crusts removed, place between two layers of cling film and roll out the bread until thin.

Next, carefully cut the bread into the desired shape, take extra care to make them uniform, it's the little details that make the difference!

On a baking tray, lay the bread between two pieces of baking paper, top with another tray and bake in the oven at 190°c until crisp.

Spinach, avocado and prawn

Serves 4

This dish is another example of something simple looking spectacular. My advice is take care when slicing the avocado, making sure it is as uniform as possible and be patient and precise when plating.

INGREDIENTS

For the spinach purée

2 bags washed spinach

Iced water

1g xanthan gum, optional but will achieve better results

Sea salt

For the avocado and prawns

½ avocado per person, sliced

1 large lemon, juiced

1 tbsp olive oil

Peeled tiger prawns, depending on size allow 4-6 per person

1 clove garlic, crushed

1 red chilli, de-seeded, diced

Sea salt

White pepper

Baby spinach

Swiss chard

METHOD

For the spinach purée

First of all, you will see I'm using xanthan gum here. This is an easily accessible ingredient that you'll find online and is a valuable commodity that helps bind your sauces or purées to stop them bleeding over your plate. This will provide a professional finish to your dishes.

Fill a large saucepan with water, season well and bring it to the boil. Add the spinach and cook for 20–30 seconds. Immediately add into the iced water to stop the cooking process and stir it around to ensure even cooling. Now add the spinach and 1g of xanthan gum to a food processor. You may need to add a little of the iced water but take your time, always remember you cannot take it back out. Once you have a smooth purée push it through a sieve to remove any bits of spinach and then add to a squeezy bottle to serve.

For the avocado and prawns

Neatly slice the avocado and toss it in the lemon juice to stop it discolouring.

In large frying pan on a medium heat add the oil. Once it is hot add the prawns and stir for around 90 seconds. Next add the garlic and chilli and cook for another 3 minutes. Once cooked, season with sea salt and white pepper and set aside.

Carefully plate the dish in a line along the centre of the plate. Start with the prawns then the avocado, carefully place the spinach leaf and the chard before finally adding the purée in neat dots along the edges the finished dish.

For an interesting twist you can add balsamic bacon (page 176) and the panna gratta (page 180) to enhance this dish.

Goat's cheese and beetroot salad

Serves 4

This visually stunning dish relies on the colours and varieties of the different types of beetroot, so be picky when you're shopping to find the best produce available.

INGREDIENTS

200g baby purple beetroot
Olive oil
Smoked sea salt
Belazu balsamic vinegar
1 candy striped beetroot
1 golden heritage beetroot
Ice water
Beetroot leaves
300g hard goat's cheese
Cracked black pepper

METHOD

For the panna gratta
Take a stale ciabatta and either chop or use a process or to break down into small bite size pieces and crumbs.

In a large frying pan add 3 tablespoons of oil and heat gently. With your knife crush a garlic clove just enough crack it open and fry off until just brown. At that point remove it from the oil and add in the breadcrumbs. Coat evenly and season with sea salt. Once they are starting to brown put them on a baking tray and toast gently in the oven for 10 minutes at 150°c until dry and crunchy. These will keep for months in an airtight container.

For the roasted baby beets
Preheat your oven to 190°c.
Clean the baby purple beetroot, remove the root tip and cut off the stem and leaves. Set these aside for your garnish later.
Toss the purple beetroots in olive oil and smoked sea salt and place into a roasting tray in the oven until softened. Check them after 45 minutes to an hour then remove them from the oven. Once cool enough to handle scrape the skin off with a paring knife and dress in the Belazu balsamic vinegar. Next, very carefully peel the candy stripe and golden beetroots and using a mandoline slice around 4 pieces per person. Next take a 2.5cm cutter and cut a perfect circle out of the beetroot slices.
Set these aside and boil a saucepan of salted water. Tidy the ends of the beetroot leaves and blanch for 30 seconds before dropping them into iced water. This will stop them cooking and keep that great colour.
Drain the beetroot leaves on some kitchen paper and start to plate up, make sure you alternate the different varieties of beetroot.
If you buy a good quality goat's cheese you only need a little and it is perfect as it is. Use a small baller to create small spheres of the cheese and then arrange around the beetroot.
Add a twist of black pepper and finish the dish by piping dots of the balsamic vinegar around the beetroot and goat's cheese.

Stilton and walnut pâté with Port and Melba toasts

Serves 4

With the classic flavours of Stilton, walnut and Port you can't really go wrong. It's a combination that's often reserved for the festive season but I think it works well for any time of the year.

INGREDIENTS

For the pâté

225g Stilton cheese

50g unsalted butter, softened

75g walnuts

For the Port chutney

2 red onions, finely chopped

2 tbsp olive oil

Pinch salt

80g light brown sugar

100ml Port

80ml Belazu balsamic vinegar

For the Melba toasts

2 slices of white bread

For the garnish

25g walnuts, to garnish

Rocket

METHOD

For the pâté

In a food processor combine the Stilton cheese and butter. Chop the walnuts by hand and then add to a bowl with the pâté mixture and combine. Add a layer of cling film to the inside of a chefs ring and then press in half of the mixture (or until the ring is a third full), then place into the fridge to set.

For the Port chutney

In a saucepan, without colouring gently soften the onions in the olive oil with the salt. Once softened add the sugar and cook for another minute before adding the Port. Reduce until thick and sticky, then add the Belazu vinegar and reduce further. Remember this will thicken once cooled.

Once it is cooled add a layer on to the top of the pâté before topping off with the remaining pâté mixture.

Carefully fold over the cling film and leave in the fridge for 30 minutes to set, or until required.

For the Melba toasts

These are simple to make and with a little extra effort can look visually stunning on this dish.

Take a rolling pin and some white bread with the crusts removed, place between two layers of cling film and roll out the bread until thin.

Next, carefully cut the bread into the desired shape, take extra care to make them uniform, remember it's those little details that make the difference!

On a baking tray, lay the bread between two pieces of baking paper, top with another tray and bake in the oven at 190°c until crisp.

For the garnish

In a dry frying pan toast the remaining walnuts, and roughly chop.

Use a hot knife to quarter the pâté and delicately plate using the toast and rocket to add height and contrast to the dish.

Pasta

How to make perfect pasta

A lot of people are nervous when it comes to making their own pasta, you shouldn't be; it's two ingredients and a lot of fun! You can buy a decent pasta machine from places like Lakeland, John Lewis and Marks and Spencer for around £25. You'll be surprised how often you use it!

Just a little bit of effort goes a long way to impressing your guests, all you need is some good quality type 00 pasta flour and some fresh free range eggs. I work on the ratio of 100g flour to one egg, but always keep one of each just in case as not all eggs are the same size.

You can make this on a board by hand but I like to make mine in a food processor. Simply add in the egg and flour – 400g of flour and four eggs are more than enough for 4 people. Blitz it up until it resembles breadcrumbs then tip it out onto a floured work surface and bring it together with your hands. Knead for a couple of minutes to activate the gluten, then shape into a ball and cover in cling film. Leave to rest somewhere cool for around 15 minutes. This step is very important, without it the dough will break up and you will not be able to roll it out properly.

The way I 'test the rest' is to gently make an indentation into the cling filmed pasta with my finger. If you can see it start to rise back up then you are ready to roll.

Here are some simple tips to keep you out of trouble when it comes to rolling:

- Always start with a clear work surface
- Flour the work surface
- Only work with the amount of pasta you can roll or fill, as pasta does dry out quickly
- Keep the rest covered with a damp cloth, towel or cling film
- Start on the widest setting of the pasta machine and roll the pasta through 5 or 6 times, then fold it back in half each time and roll it again. What this will do is save your arms and kneed your dough for you, making it easier to work with.

That's essentially it. Don't be scared, it's great fun, cheap and tasty. Plus it cooks in just 2-3 minutes, saving you that little bit of time to enjoy your company!

1.

2.

3.

4.

5.

6.

Dried pasta and how to cook it

Cooking pasta is easy but a lot of people tend to over-cook it, ending up with it all stuck together. Here are some simple things you can do to make your life easier at dinner time!

A few essentials to have ready to go are:
- Your biggest pan – it needs to be huge
- Sea salt
- Boiling water
- A cup or mug
- A colander
- Warm bowls or plates

Fill your pan with water, pop the lid on and place it over a high heat, bringing it up to boil. Once boiling add the salt, and be generous! I sometimes cook my pasta in stock to get the advantage of additional flavour in my dish. When the water is boiling rapidly, add in the pasta, stir once and leave it to simmer away. After around 8 minutes carefully take a bit out and test it. You want it slightly al dente (Italian for 'to the tooth'). If it's a little hard wait 30 seconds and check it again, then repeat until you're happy with it.

Before you strain away your water through the colander, retain a full cup in case you need it for your sauce.

Now it's time to move fast. Strain your pasta and get it into your sauce immediately. Remember it will steam sat in the colander and you run the risk of over-cooking it. Give the pasta a good toss in the sauce and serve into warm bowls as quickly and neatly as you can. If you are cooking long pasta like tagliatelle or spaghetti, the very best way to serve it is to use tongs, and always lift it high above the pan separating each portion from the rest. I like to shape mine in a separate bowl, using tongs in a twisting motion, then move it to my serving dish. This helps to keep your finished dish looking clean and tidy.

All of these principles also apply to fresh pasta with the exception of the time. A filled pasta shape will cook in around 2-3 minutes and spaghetti in just over half that time.

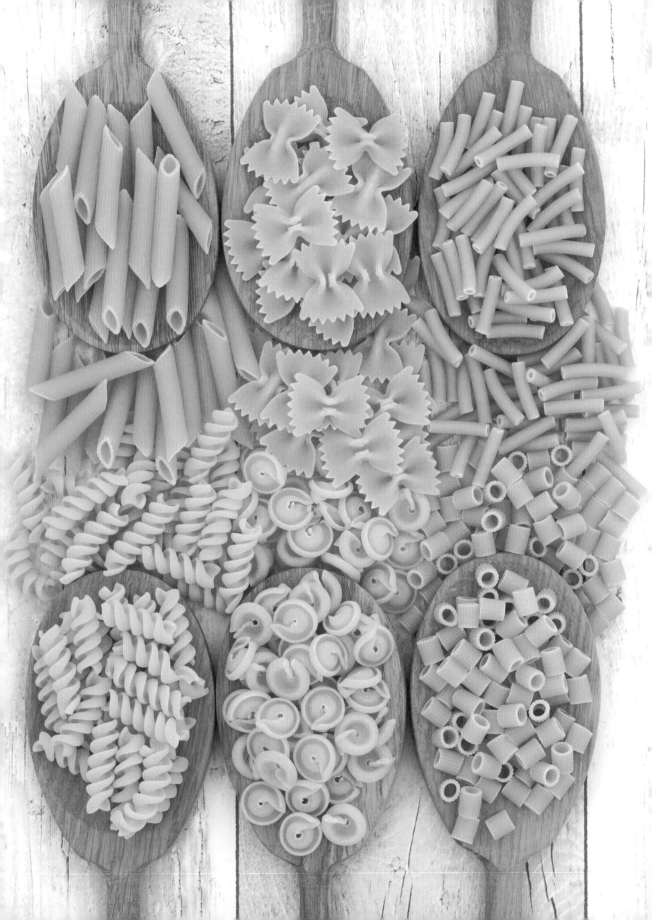

Wild mushroom ravioli with sage butter and panna gratta

Serves 4

Making your own ravioli takes a bit of effort but is absolutely worth it. The earthiness of the mushrooms combined with the silky sage butter and fresh light pasta will ensure you never reach for the store bought stuff again! Start off by making the pasta as per the recipe on page 42, then wrap in cling film and set aside to rest.

INGREDIENTS

For the pasta

100g pasta flour

2 free range eggs

For the ravioli filling

250g wild mushrooms

50g whole chestnuts, cooked and peeled

2 heaped tbsp ricotta

5 fresh sage leaves per person, plus 1 tsp for the filling

1½ tsp fresh rosemary

1½ tsp fresh thyme

2 cloves garlic, minced

Butter

Sea salt

Black pepper

To serve

Panna gratta, see page 180

METHOD

For the ravioli filling

Set aside a small selection of the wild mushrooms. Pick out the small ones to be used to garnish the dish.

Next chop together the wild mushrooms, chestnuts, ricotta and fresh herbs. Use the back of a knife to crush the garlic into a paste. Add a large knob of butter to a frying pan followed by the garlic and soften. After around 1 minute add in the mushroom mixture, stir well and gently cook through until soft. Season and then set aside to cool.

To roll

Take half of the now rested pasta, dust the work surface and flatten the dough a little with your fingers. Now start to work it through the pasta machine. Start on the widest setting, run it through a couple of times and then gradually work your way through the settings until you get to the last but one. Remember that you are going to double this up when you make the ravioli. It needs to be thin enough to not to be too dense when folded over, but thick enough to hold the filling. Cover the now rolled sheet of pasta with cling film to prevent it drying out and repeat this process with the remaining dough. On the floured work surface lay the pasta sheets next to each other. Use a heaped teaspoon to evenly place the cooled filling in two even lines along the entire length of one of the sheets of pasta. Now comes the important bit; take the remaining sheet of pasta and carefully place this on top of one end of the pasta. Using the side of your hand and little finger, gently cup and press the sheets together around the filling. Then use a pasta or a pastry cutter to finish the edges of the ravioli.

To cook

Add the ravioli to a large pan of gently boiling water. They will only take 2 minutes to cook, and once they float they are almost there. In a frying pan add a knob of butter and the carefully selected mushroom garnish. Heat until it foams and then add the sage leaves, quickly followed by the ravioli. Let a little of the pasta water go into the butter and gently swirl the pan in a circular motion to emulsify the sauce.

Serve immediately and top with a little panna gratta.

Cauliflower linguine with Parmesan tuile

Serves 4

This is my pasta version of cauliflower cheese. It looks amazing, and is the ultimate comfort food at the same time.

INGREDIENTS

200g cauliflower florets

200g Parmesan, grated for the tuiles

75g Parmesan, grated for the sauce

300g linguine, either dry or fresh see pages 40-44

100g cauliflower, to add to the sauce

Sea salt and white pepper

For the béchamel sauce

600ml milk

1 bay leaf (optional)

1 pinch fresh nutmeg, grated

60g butter

60g plain flour

Salt and freshly ground black pepper, to taste

METHOD

Boil a large pan of salted water, add the cauliflower and cook for around 8 minutes, or until soft.

For the béchamel sauce

Firstly, in a saucepan heat the milk with the bay leaf and nutmeg, taking care that it doesn't boil over.

Next melt the butter in a large saucepan over a low heat. Once melted gently sift in the flour stirring all the time until you have a thick paste. Cook the paste out, moving continuously for a couple of minutes.

Using a ladle slowly whisk in a little of the infused milk at a time, stirring continuously until you have a smooth, slightly thick sauce. Remove from the heat, and season with salt and pepper.

For the tuiles

Heat the oven to 190°c. On a non-stick baking tray use a chef's ring to make 8cm rounds of the grated cheese. Remember it will melt so make it slightly thicker than you need. Place in the oven for 5 minutes and watch them all the time to make sure they don't burn.

Remove from the oven and allow to cool. You can cut out a neater shape once almost cooled with a slightly smaller cutter.

Next add the béchamel sauce to a food processor with 100g of the cooked cauliflower and the rest of the Parmesan. Blitz until you have a smooth consistency.

Cook the pasta according to the instructions in the recipe on page 42-44 and then add it to the sauce, combining the two well. Add the remaining cauliflower florets and combine.

Now delicately plate the linguine using tongues, gently placing the tuile on an angle on top with a sprinkling of white pepper.

Penne primavera

Serves 4

Make the most of spring vegetables at their best with this light pasta dish. You can buy the pesto, but I'd recommend making my recipe for the freshest and most flavoursome outcome.

INGREDIENTS

75g dry penne, cooked according to the recipe on page 44

30g peeled broad beans

8 sugar snap peas

50g petits pois

4 asparagus spears per person

Ice water

Butter, for frying

Pesto, see page 188

Sea salt and white pepper

Micro basil

Pea shoots

For the pesto

50g pine nuts

2 cloves garlic

Pinch sea salt

2 large bunches basil

50g Parmesan

150ml olive oil

½ lemon, juiced

METHOD

For the pesto

In a large frying pan toast the pine nuts until golden.

Next use the back of your knife to crush the garlic into a smooth paste. A little sea salt will help to do this.

I make my pesto in a food processor, but you can use a pestle and mortar. With the exception of the lemon juice add in all the remaining ingredients and blitz into a smooth paste. Taste and add the lemon juice and adjust the seasoning accordingly.

For the penne

Boil two large pans of salted water.

Cook the pasta in one of them according to the instructions in the recipe on page 44.

In the other pan blanch each set of vegetables and drop them into the iced water to stop the cooking process. Once cool remove and dry on kitchen paper. You can use frozen peas for this but simply let them defrost, there is no need to blanch them.

Next in a frying pan add a knob of butter and 2 tablespoons of pesto per person. Add in the pasta and combine well.

Meanwhile in another frying pan, heat up a knob of butter and add the blanched vegetables and warm them through. You don't need to cook them too much. Season and get ready to serve.

Place your penne in the centre of the plate and use this as a base on which to show off your vegetables. Top with pea shoots and any remaining pesto and serve while hot.

Charred vegetable conchiglie

Serves 4

This quick pasta dish is ideal for a midweek dinner after a long day. Griddling the vegetables provides an irresistible sweet, succulent and slightly charred flavour that you just don't get when steaming or boiling.

INGREDIENTS

90g courgette per person

4 baby aubergines

Olive oil

2 red peppers

2 yellow peppers

1 clove garlic, crushed

300g dry conchiglie

5 tbsp pesto, see below

Fresh oregano

Micro basil

Sea salt and white pepper

For the pesto

50g pine nuts

2 cloves garlic

Pinch sea salt

2 large bunches basil

50g Parmesan

150ml olive oil

½ lemon, juiced

METHOD

For the pesto

In a large frying pan toast the pine nuts until golden.

Next use the back of your knife to crush the garlic into a smooth paste. A little sea salt will help to do this.

I make my pesto in a food processor, but you can use a pestle and mortar. With the exception of the lemon juice add in all the remaining ingredients and blitz into a smooth paste. Taste and add the lemon juice and adjust the seasoning accordingly.

For the conchiglie

Quarter the courgettes and aubergines and brush with olive oil. Use a hot griddle pan to scorch the white flesh, and set aside.

Next dice the peppers and sauté with the garlic in a frying pan with a little olive oil.

Bring a large pan of salted water to the boil and cook the pasta according to the instructions in the recipe on page 42-44.

Add a knob of butter to a frying pan then add the pesto and pasta, combining well.

At the same time add the courgettes and aubergines to the other frying pan and heat through.

Plate carefully by placing the conchiglie in the centre of the plate. Use this as a base on which to show off your vegetables, and then top with oregano and micro basil and season to taste.

Chicken and chorizo tortellini

Serves 4

These impressive and highly flavoured pasta parcels are a great addition to any cook's repertoire. They look great, they freeze great, and they taste even better! Top it all off and serve with a pancetta crisp.
I'm serving these in my classic tomato sauce found on page 185.

INGREDIENTS

300g pasta, see page 42

For the filling

150g chorizo sausage, diced

2 chicken breasts

1 tsp smoked paprika

1 tbsp olive oil

30g fresh basil, chopped

3 tbsp ricotta

Sea salt

Black pepper

For the pancetta crisps

1 slice pancetta per person

To garnish

Pea shoots

tomato sauce, see page 185

METHOD

For the filling

Take a frying pan and gently fry off the chorizo to release its oil with all of that amazing smoky flavour. Once gently browned and starting to crisp, set aside to cool. In a food processor, add the chicken breast, smoked paprika, olive oil, fresh basil, 2 tablespoons of ricotta, salt, pepper, cooled chorizo and its oil. Blitz the mixture into a smooth paste.

For the tortellini

I make my tortellini with round pasta wrappers. Something to remember here is to make sure the dough is rolled as thinly as possible and don't over fill your pasta.

Using my fresh pasta method on page 42 roll out a length of dough that is a manageable amount for you to work with. Using a 3 inch round cutter, cut the dough into circles, spacing the circles as close together as possible to get as much out of your dough as you can. Next, place 1 teaspoon of filling in the middle of each round of pasta. Have a little bowl of water to dip your finger in to seal them. Wet your finger and run it along the edge of the pasta circle to moisten it. Fold the dough over to form a half moon, taking care to seal from right to left to squeeze out as much air as possible. Next, draw the two corners together to form a bucket. Press them securely together to seal. Place the parcel on a baking tray covered with flour, set it aside, cover and then repeat.

For the pancetta crisps

You will need one slice of pancetta per person, two baking trays and two pieces of baking paper. Lay one piece of your paper on top of one of the trays, place the pancetta on to it and top again with greaseproof paper. Top with the other baking tray and roast in the oven at 190°c until firm and crisp, usually after around 7 minutes.

To plate

Drop the tortellini in a pan of boiling salted water for 3-4 minutes. Set aside on a J-cloth while you plate up the sauce. Then carefully add the pasta followed by the bacon crisp. Finally dress the plate with pea shoots and serve.

Pan-fried gnocchi with steak and green pesto

Serves 4

This is my more refined version of the British favourite of steak and chips. The steak has been carefully sliced and plated rather than presented in one large piece, and instead of thick bland chips I've made fresh gnocchi. The herby pesto and crispy rosemary add that extra bit of texture and flavour to really set things off.

INGREDIENTS

For the gnocchi
400g red potatoes
400g plain flour
1 large egg
White pepper
Salt
Ice

For the steak
170–200g fillet steak per person
Olive oil
Rosemary
Butter, for frying
Pesto

METHOD

For the gnocchi
Roast the potatoes at 190°c. Let them cool a little and then scoop out the inside then mash. You do not need to add anything to the mash, keep it as dry as possible. Bring a large pan of salted water to the boil.

Next add the flour, egg and seasoning to the mash and work into a dry dough. Divide the mixture into 4 equal parts and roll out into a sausage shape, around 20mm in diameter. Use a plastic spatula to cut the gnocchi at 25mm intervals. Remember be neat and precise, a little care will make a huge difference when it comes to plating the dish.

Get a large bowl with iced water ready and in small batches drop the gnocchi into the boiling water. Once they float they are cooked. Remove them and stop the cooking process by dropping them into the iced water. In a colander toss them in a little olive oil to stop them sticking and place them on a baking tray lined with greaseproof paper. Cover with some cling film ready to crisp up in a frying pan at the last minute.

For the steak
If you have the equipment you can sous vide the steak. With this, it will take 1 hour at 53°c to get a perfect medium rare steak. After 60 minutes remove the steak and dry on a J-cloth, then rub with a little olive oil and season with sea salt. Alternatively, pan fry to your liking.

Now it's time to bring the dish together. Take two large frying pans and add a little olive oil to one of them. Once hot, add the rosemary, fry until crisp then remove and set aside. In the same pan add the gnocchi and a knob of butter and cook until golden and warm throughout, adding the baby chard 30 seconds from the end of cooking. Next in a hot pan add a little colour to your steak; this only takes a second, so make sure you do not overcook your meat. Add a knob of butter and heat up, next add the steak and using a spoon baste the foaming butter over the top. This should only take 20-30 seconds each side. Set the steak aside and rest for a minimum of 2 minutes. Now it's time to carefully plate the dish. Make sure the fillet is well rested on a J-cloth; this will prevent blood and juices leaking out and spoiling the finished plate. Neatly slice the steak and arrange surrounded by a few of the gnocchi and the crispy rosemary. Finish with a drizzle of pesto.

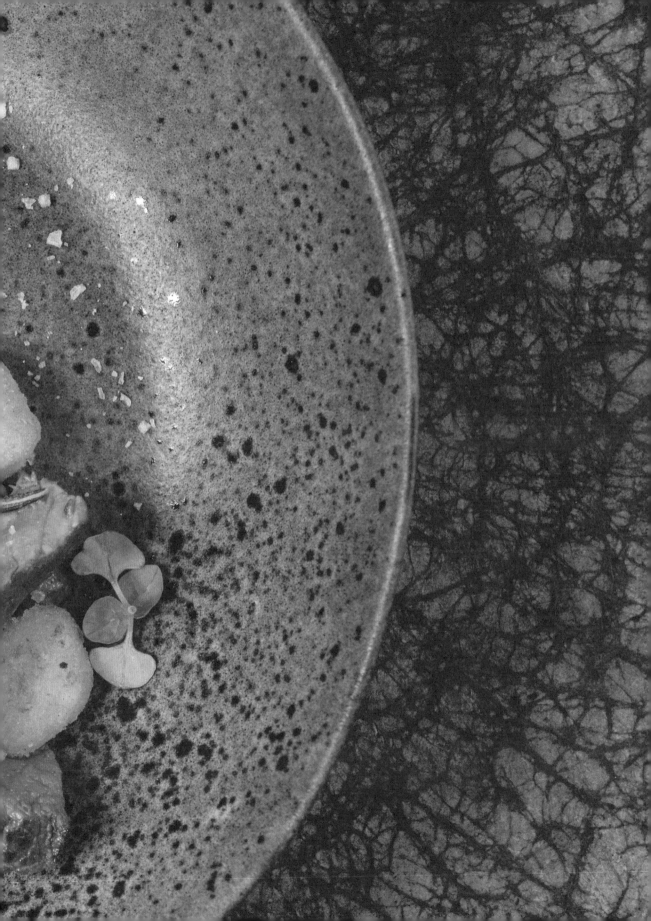

Marvellous mac 'n' cheese

Mac 'n' cheese does have the tendency to split sometimes and become oily. The way you can avoid that is with sodium citrate, which is readily available online.

INGREDIENTS

For the mac 'n' cheese
480g macaroni pasta, dried
265ml whole milk
11g sodium citrate
200g mature cheddar cheese, grated
100g Parmesan, grated
Sea salt and white pepper
½ clove garlic, finely minced
½ tsp English mustard powder
3 fine grates of fresh nutmeg

For the bon-bons
75g panna gratta blended
1 tsp smoked paprika
75g panna gratta crumbed

For the garnish
Popcorn shoots (optional)
Micro basil
Smoked paprika

METHOD

For the sauce
You can make this the day before. In a large saucepan over a medium heat combine the milk and sodium citrate and whisk until dissolved. Bit by bit, slowly add both the cheddar and Parmesan cheese and melt. Add the garlic, mustard powder and nutmeg. Blend each addition with a stick blender until the sauce is silky and smooth. Make sure that you taste and season well. Keep in the fridge until needed.

For the mac 'n' cheese bon-bons, make this the day before

Cook 240g macaroni pasta (this makes 8 bon-bons) according to the dry pasta method found on page 44, this is for the pasta bon-bons.

Warm through half of the sauce and add in the pasta along with 75g of the panna gratta that you have blitzed in a processor. Add a heaped teaspoon of smoked paprika, mix well and chill in the fridge overnight.

When ready to make the mac 'n' cheese bon-bons, remove the pre-made mac and cheese from the fridge and shape into evenly sized balls. Once rounded, roll in the remaining panna gratta breadcrumbs. Pop them in the freezer for 10 minutes to firm up and then remove and check the shape, if you need to perfect them they will be easier to manage now.

Finally, deep fry at 190°c until golden brown and warmed throughout. This will take around 3 minutes.

Drain on paper towels.

For the mac 'n' cheese
Cook 240g macaroni pasta according to the dry pasta method found on page 44.

Warm through the remainder of the sauce and combine with the cooked pasta.

To plate
Add the mac 'n' cheese to the plate, dust with paprika and serve alongside the deep-fried bon-bons and garnish with some basil and popcorn shoots which will add a sweet buttery flavour.

Tagliatelle verde with pork and herb mascarpone meatballs

Serves 4

Meatballs are versatile, easy to make and perfect for storing as they keep very well in the freezer. You don't have to serve them with pasta; these meatballs are delicious on a warm ciabatta roll. I'm serving these with my pesto sauce.

INGREDIENTS

For the pasta
300g 00 pasta flour

3 free range eggs

75g cooked spinach

For the meatballs
300g pork mince

300g beef mince

1 tsp dried oregano

1 tbsp fresh oregano, chopped

50g bread crumbs

75g ricotta

Sea salt and white pepper

Olive oil, for frying

For the pesto
50g pine nuts

2 cloves garlic

Pinch sea salt

Two large bunches basil

50g Parmesan

150ml olive oil

½ lemon, juiced

For the garnish
Parmesan

Pea shoots

Baby chard

METHOD

For the pesto
In a large frying pan toast the pine nuts until golden.

Next use the back of your knife to crush the garlic into a smooth paste. A little sea salt will help to do this. I make my pesto in a food processor, but you can use a pestle and mortar. With the exception of the lemon juice add in all the remaining ingredients and blitz into a smooth paste. Taste and add the lemon juice and adjust the seasoning accordingly.

For the pasta
Fill a large saucepan with water. Season well and bring it to the boil, then add in the spinach. Cook for 20–30 seconds then immediately put into a bowl of iced water to stop the cooking process. Stir it around to ensure even cooling. When cool remove from the water, squeeze in a towel until dry and then place in the bowl of a food processor. Purée until a very fine paste forms.

Add 3 eggs to the food processor and blend. Then add the pasta flour and blitz it up until it resembles a crumble. You may need to add a little more egg or flour to get the consistency right.

Empty the crumble mixture out onto a floured work surface and bring it together with your hands. Knead it for a couple of minutes to activate the gluten, then roll it into a ball and cover in cling film. Rest for around 15 minutes.

Roll out, cut and cook according to the instructions on page 42.

For the meatballs
Combine all of the ingredients in a large mixing bowl. Use a large serving spoon to mix well and then roll them onto balls with wet hands.

Add a little olive oil to a large frying pan followed by the meatballs and gently fry until browned and cooked through. This will take around 10–12 minutes. Drain off any excess fat, set aside and add leave to rest for 3 minutes.

In another frying pan add some olive oil and 2 tablespoons of pesto per person. Add the pasta and combine before topping with the meatballs and a generous shaving of Parmesan, pea shoots and baby chard.

Tagliatelle carbonara with bacon crisps

Serves 4

No pasta section of a recipe book would be complete without a creamy carbonara. My version has bacon crisps to create a bit of added texture.

INGREDIENTS

300g tagliatelle

100g diced pancetta

1 slice pancetta per person

3 medium eggs

5 tbsp single cream

3 tbsp ricotta cheese

4 tbsp finely grated Parmesan cheese

Sea salt and freshly ground white pepper

Small basil leaves

METHOD

Bring a large saucepan of lightly salted water to the boil. Add the pasta and cook according to the instructions on page 44.

Meanwhile, in a dry frying pan gently fry the pancetta until it has browned and the fat cooks out, and then drain on some kitchen paper.

For the bacon crisps you will need one slice of pancetta per person, two baking trays and two pieces of baking paper. Lay one piece of paper on top of one of the trays, place the pancetta onto it and top again with greaseproof paper. Top with the other baking tray and roast in the oven at 190°c until firm and crisp. This will usually take around 7 minutes.

In a bowl mix together the eggs, single cream, ricotta and half of the Parmesan. Season a little – take care with the salt as the pancetta will naturally add salt to the dish.

Drain the pasta, retaining a little of the cooking water, then gently stir in the cream and egg mixture. You need to do this off the heat otherwise you'll get scrambled eggs.

Stir in the pancetta, then divide between four serving bowls and sprinkle with the remaining Parmesan. Top with a bacon crisp, some carefully selected small basil leaves and add a pinch of white pepper.

Non-Gluten

Harissa lamb cutlets with sweet potato, pomegranate and almonds

Serves 4

The North African spices in the harissa paste bring out a beautiful flavour from this cut of lamb. The sweet potato and pomegranate seeds will balance out the heat whilst the almonds provide a pleasing crunch.

INGREDIENTS

For the harissa paste
10 red chillies

1 tsp caraway seeds

1 tsp coriander seeds

3-4 garlic cloves, minced

½ tsp sea salt

1 tsp paprika

50ml olive oil

For the lamb
Rack of lamb, French trimmed, 3 cutlets per person

For the sweet potato
4 large sweet potatoes

Olive oil

Salt and pepper

For the garnish
1 pomegranate, seeds

20 whole almonds

½ tsp smoked paprika

½ tsp honey

Micro coriander

METHOD

Preheat your oven to 200°c.

For the harissa paste
Chop and de-seed the red chillies. In a large dry frying pan heat the caraway and coriander seeds and then pound in a pestle and mortar. Using a food processor blitz the chillies and garlic cloves into a paste, then add in the toasted and ground seeds, salt, paprika and olive oil. Blitz into a smooth paste then cook off in a frying pan on a medium heat for around 3 minutes.

For the lamb
In a large frying pan sear the lamb making sure all of the exposed meat and fat is browned. Next generously coat the lamb with half of the harissa paste and place in the oven for around 12 minutes. Remove and check the internal temperature with a meat thermometer. It should be around 63°c. Coat the meat again with the rest of the harissa and leave to rest.

For the sweet potato
Slice the potatoes into 2cm thick slices and then using a 3cm round cutter cut out 3 rounds of sweet potato per person. Drizzle with olive oil, season and roast in the oven for around 15 minutes at 190°c.

For the garnish
Halve and de-seed the pomegranate using the back of a spoon to knock the seeds out. In a dry frying pan add in the almonds and smoked paprika. Toast them off and remove from the heat adding a little squeeze of honey.

To plate
Carve the lamb and leave on a J-cloth to rest. Plate standing up alongside the potatoes. Add the micro coriander, sweet sticky almonds and finally the pomegranate pearls to give the dish that vibrant colour.

Pan-seared sea bass with cauliflower, sweet potato and zucchini fritti

Serves 4

The textured, juicy seabass is the star of the show here, so make sure you're discerning with the fillets you buy. The different purées look wonderful when dotted on the plate and the zucchini fritti is that extra element that, whilst a bit fiddly to make, takes the dish to the next level.

INGREDIENTS

For the sea bass
40g butter
Salt and pepper, to taste
1 x 140g sea bass fillet per person

For the cauliflower purée
1 cauliflower, roughly chopped
20ml double cream
20g butter

For the sweet potato purée
1kg peeled sweet potatoes
125ml double cream
125ml milk

For the zucchini fritti
1 large egg, lightly beaten
Ice-cold water
200g plain gluten-free flour, double sifted
Fresh oregano

METHOD

For the sea bass
In a large frying pan add the butter and let it start to foam. Score, season and then place the sea bass skin side down. Cook for 2½ minutes. Turn the fish so the skin side faces up and remove the pan from the heat. Let the fish finish cooking in the residual heat for 30 seconds, remove and rest.

For the cauliflower purée
Place the chopped cauliflower into a food processor and pulse 3-4 times. Scrape down the sides of the bowl and pulse again. Transfer to a saucepan and gently soften in the cream for around 5 minutes stirring regularly. Add the butter and seasoning and cook for another 5 minutes. Transfer it back into the processor and blend for 1 minute until smooth.

For the sweet potato purée
Peel and cut the potatoes in small cubes around 1cm square. Add to a saucepan along with the cream and the milk, season and cook until softened. Once cooked let it cool a little and then add into the processor and blend for 2 minutes until smooth.

For the zucchini fritti
I use a spiraliser to make these, they can be a little fiddly but they are worth the extra effort. Make a courgette noodle and set aside to make your batter. To do this pour the beaten egg into a measuring jug and add enough icy cold water to make the volume up to 275ml. Pour into a large mixing bowl and then add the flour and mix roughly.

Dip your courgette noodles in the batter and then in a lightly oiled cold frying pan curl the noodle round to make a spiral disc. Place them over the heat and allow them to crisp up, just before turning, brush a little more of the batter and flip over to brown until golden on both sides.

To plate
I like to use squeezy bottles for my purées as you get a more professional look to your dish. Evenly space the purées alongside your fish, alternating in type. Add the fritti and garnish with fresh oregano.

Soy seared tuna with sesame egg noodles, spring onions and chilli

Serves 4

This is a really quick lunch or tasting menu dish that is packed with flavour and looks incredible. It takes literally minutes to cook so it's always a good dish to have up your sleeve. I accidentally came across the egg noodles element of the dish when I used sesame oil instead of olive oil one morning, and I think it adds a beautiful extra layer of flavour. I use micro coriander in this dish but there is no reason why you can't use its grown up equivalent.

INGREDIENTS

For the tuna

1 x 200g tuna steak per person

1 tbsp olive oil

Kikkoman soy sauce, gluten-free

1 spring onion per person

½ red chilli per person

For the egg noodles

1 large free range egg per person

2 tsp sesame oil

1 tbsp olive oil

1 clove garlic, peeled

Sesame seeds

Micro coriander

METHOD

Firstly, let the tuna come to room temperature and rub each side with olive oil and a dash of soy sauce and roll in the sesame seeds. Use a mandoline or a very sharp knife to cut the chilli on the angle. Slice the spring onions the same as thinly as you can. It's important they are thin as you don't want to overpower any other element on the dish.

In a jug beat the eggs one at a time and then add the sesame oil before beating again. In a good quality dry non-stick frying pan over a medium heat add in the egg. Use a swirling motion to make a thin layer of egg pancake, there's no need to toss it, just let it cook through gently and then set aside. Cook the next one and layer them up separating them with baking paper.

In a hot frying pan add in the olive oil, then smash the peeled garlic clove with the back of your knife. Fry it off in the oil to infuse with the garlic flavour.

Remove the garlic before it goes too dark and bitter, then using some tongs quickly sear each side and the edges of your tuna, for no more than 10 seconds per side. Season with soy sauce and set it aside to rest.

Use a very sharp knife to slice the tuna as thinly as possible; it should be nice and pink inside with a ring around the edges where you have seared it.

In the same frying pan as the tuna, quickly warm through one of the pancakes and then on a chopping board roll it into a cigar shape. As thinly as you can with your sharpest knife, slice it into noodles, and repeat for the rest of the pancakes.

Dress the plate with the noodles in a zig zag style and interweave the tuna slices, top with the chilli, spring onions and micro coriander. Add a little splash of soy and serve.

Pork belly with marvellous mash, broad beans and asparagus

Serves 4

The pork in this dish I have cooked sous vide at 82°c for 18 hours, I find this provides the best result. If you don't have this equipment, you can roast it slowly on a wire rack for 4½ hours at 150°c. You will need to do this the day before so that you can press and portion it.

INGREDIENTS

100g pork belly per person

For the marvellous mash

1kg red potatoes, peeled, cubed

100ml double cream

400g unsalted butter, diced

Sea salt

White pepper

For the broad beans and asparagus

50g broad beans

3 asparagus spears per person

Iced water

METHOD

For the pork belly

Once the pork belly is cooked as per the instructions above, lay it between two pieces of baking paper and press between two baking trays. Weigh it down (I use tins from my cupboard) and then chill in the fridge overnight. The next day you can remove the jellified stock and set aside in a small saucepan. Reduce this over a high heat before serving with your finished dish.

Next portion the pork neatly before gently pan frying until golden on all sides ready for service.

For the marvellous mash

Boil the potatoes in well salted water until soft. Drain over the sink in a colander and then place a clean tea towel over the top. This will draw any moisture into it leaving you with fluffy, steamed dry potatoes.

In a saucepan on a low heat add the cream and butter, 1½ teaspoons of sea salt and a really good twist of white pepper and gently melt.

If you have a ricer pass your potato through it onto a saucepan over a very low heat. Now start to ladle your mixture one ladle at a time onto your potato, whisking until incorporated. Check your seasoning and set aside.

For the broad beans and asparagus

Peel the broad beans and stems of asparagus.

Fill a large saucepan with water, season well and bring it to the boil. Add the broad beans and asparagus and cook for 1 minute. Immediately add into the iced water to stop the cooking process and stir them around to ensure even cooling. Once cool remove and dry on kitchen paper or a J-cloth. To serve, add a little butter to a frying pan, season with salt and then heat through.

To plate

Pipe the mash to get a good presentation style; it can be hot so pop some gloves on if needed. Plate the sliced pork belly alongside the mash, finish with your greens and reduced jus then serve immediately.

Crispy chicken rillettes with softened Camembert and beetroot chutney

Serves 4

This is a great alternative to a cheese board and would work well either before or after a meal. Instead of piling the chutney on the plate, I like to blitz it into a paste and then pipe it delicately next to the cheese and rillettes.

INGREDIENTS

For the chicken rillettes

3 rashers smoked streaky bacon, minced

2 shallots, diced

75g chestnut mushrooms, minced

500g skin on chicken thighs

Olive oil

Sea salt

White pepper

1 tsp fresh thyme

50g butter

1 tbsp ricotta

For the cheese

1 Camembert round

Olive oil

For the chutney

300g beetroot, chopped

Olive oil

1 red onion, grated

2 Granny Smith apples, peeled and grated

200g red wine vinegar

½ tsp sea salt

75g brown sugar

1 candy striped beetroot

METHOD

Preheat your oven to 190°c.

For the chicken rillettes

Place a little butter in a frying pan then add the bacon. Add the shallots and gently soften, then add the mushrooms and cook until softened. Set aside to cool. Drizzle the chicken thighs with olive oil and season well with sea salt and white pepper. Roast in the oven for 30 minutes.

Let the chicken cool a little, remove the skin and then shred the meat either by hand or with two forks. Take care to chop the skin with a sharp knife into small pieces. Now take half of the chicken meat, all of the skin, shallots and mushrooms and blitz in a food processor. Add the butter, ricotta and thyme, making sure you reserve a couple of leaves, then blitz again. Add this paste to the remaining shredded chicken and press into moulds or individual ramekins. Chill in the fridge.

For the cheese

Remove any plastic packaging from the cheese and place back in its box, leaving the lid off. Pierce the top of the cheese in several places with a sharp knife and press some thyme into the holes. Place on a baking sheet, then brush with olive oil. Bake in the oven until the centre of the cheese has melted (approximately 10 minutes).

For the chutney

Wearing gloves peel and chop 300g beetroot, drizzle with a little olive oil and then roast in the oven at 190°c until softened. Remove and leave to cool. In a frying pan add a little olive oil followed by the onion and soften. Add in the apple and cook for 2 minutes, stirring continuously.

Next add the beetroot, apple and onion to a food processor and pulse gently until almost a paste, but not quite.

Return to the frying pan and add the red wine vinegar, salt and sugar and bring to the boil for 20 minutes, stirring regularly.

Remove from the heat and set aside to cool.

Use a mandoline to thinly slice the candy stripe beetroot and a circle cutter to cut out for the garnish.

Plate your dish as per the picture and enjoy!

BBQ ribs and coleslaw

Serves 4

Everyone loves ribs but trying to make them look presentable on a plate can be tricky, so I've provided a few quick tips on how to best do this, I hope you enjoy it!

I like to sous vide my bacon ribs for 18 hours at 82°c, but you can cover them in foil, add 200ml water to a roasting tray and cook them in the oven at 150°c for 4 hours.

INGREDIENTS

For the BBQ sauce

3 tsp olive oil

1 red onion, grated

1 red chilli

2 cloves garlic, minced

1 tsp smoked paprika

50g Dijon mustard

100g Demerara sugar

50g maple syrup

50ml red wine vinegar

500ml passata

For the ribs

750g pork ribs

For the slaw

4 free-range egg yolks

2 tsp Dijon mustard

250ml vegetable oil

1 tbsp white wine vinegar

1 large carrot, spiralised

1 courgette, spiralised

½ white cabbage, shredded finely

Celery salt

Freshly ground white pepper

Micro coriander

METHOD

For the BBQ sauce

Add the olive oil to a saucepan on a medium heat and fry off the onion, chilli and garlic. Add in the paprika and coat evenly. Now add the mustard, sugar and maple syrup and stir well before adding the red wine vinegar and passata. Cook until thick and sticky and then add into a food processor and blitz until smooth.

For the ribs

Heat the water bath to 82°c and cook the ribs for 18 hours. If you don't have a water bath, use the oven method above. Once cooked remove and shred the meat, chopping it through with a knife. Coat it in the BBQ sauce and press it into a brownie tin to make a mini rib loaf.

Bake this in the oven at 190°c for 10 minutes to crisp up the edges. Brush with the extra BBQ sauce and serve.

For the slaw

Place the egg yolks in a large, clean bowl and add the mustard and vinegar. Whisk until combined and very, very slowly add a small amount of the oil and whisk until it's well blended in. Keep going and steadily add a little more oil and whisk again and again until you have a nice thick creamy mayonnaise. Combine this with the spiralised carrot, courgette and shredded cabbage. Season with celery salt and pepper, then twist into a mound and sprinkle with coriander to serve.

Mole chicken with holy guacamole

Serves 4

Mexican food is tricky to plate and look refined, but with this mole sauce and chicken ballotine stuffed with refried beans I will show you how you can make that happen.

For this recipe you will need to make my holy guacamole, which can be found on page 179.

INGREDIENTS

For the tortillas

150g gluten free masa harina flour

Sea salt

100ml cold water

Olive oil

For the mole

2 dried ancho chillies

30g cocoa

30g dark chocolate, 85%

3 cloves garlic, peeled

500ml passata

1 onion

50g unsalted peanuts

1 tbsp smoked paprika

1 tsp ground cumin

½ tsp cinnamon

1 tsp chilli powder

For the chicken

400g pinto beans

1 clove garlic, peeled

Sea salt

White pepper

25g butter

4 chicken breasts

12 slices of Parma ham

Micro coriander

METHOD

For the tortillas

In a bowl mix the masa harina flour with the salt and slowly add the water and a tablespoon of olive oil. Combine until you have smooth dough then rest in the fridge for 5 minutes. Roll the dough into small balls and then cook the tortillas in a lightly oiled frying pan over a high heat. For quality presentation take extra care to cut the tortillas into even narrow triangular shapes.

For the mole

In a food processor soften the dried ancho chillies in boiling water. Then add in the rest of the mole ingredients and blitz until smooth. Transfer to a saucepan and cook out the sauce until thick and sticky.

For the chicken

Blitz the pinto beans with a garlic clove, sea salt, white pepper and the butter. Fry in a pan until cooked through and then set aside to cool.

Next butterfly the chicken breast by making a cut sideways along the middle of the breast and open it out like a book. Place this between two sheets of cling film and beat with a rolling pin until flat.

On a double length of cling film lay out your Parma ham and top with your flattened chicken breast. Add in a generous amount of the cooled refried beans. Roll this tightly into a ballotine, and secure the ends of the cling film with a knot.

Poach in boiling water for 15 minutes, remove and set aside to rest for 5 minutes before unwrapping and browning off in a frying pan. Level the ends up before slicing on the angle so it will stand up on the plate.

Add this to the centre of a wide round plate and garnish with the mole sauce, holy guacamole, tortilla triangles and coriander.

Turkey with bravas and a pea and onion fricassee

Serves 4

For this recipe I am going to use sous vide equipment to cook the turkey breast. It is an easy meat to dry out and this style of cooking eliminates any risk of that. If you don't have a sous vide you can cover in butter and garlic and add 100ml of water to the bottom of a roasting tray. Cook it in the oven at 180°c, basting regularly with the juices for 40 minutes.

INGREDIENTS

700g turkey breast per person
30g butter
Pinch sea salt
6 cloves garlic

For the bravas

100g red potatoes per person
Olive oil
5 cloves garlic
1 tbsp smoked paprika
2 red chillies, roughly chopped

For the pea and onion fricassee

2 red onions per person, thinly sliced
Chorizo crumb oil, see page 178
25g butter
4 tsp chorizo crumb, see page 178
Pinch sea salt
Petits pois
Pinch white pepper

METHOD

For the turkey

Remove the skin from the turkey breast (reserve the skin to make turkey crackling) and portion each serving accurately. Package with 25g of the butter, sea salt and the garlic, then set aside ready to place in the water bath. Heat up the sous vide to 65°c, place the sealed turkey parcels into the bath and cook for 2 hours.

For the turkey crackling

You'll need two baking trays and two pieces of baking paper. Gently rub a little oil onto the skin and season with sea salt. Lay one piece of the paper on top of one of the trays, place the turkey skin onto it and top again with greaseproof paper. Top with the next baking tray and roast in the oven at 190°c until firm and crisp, usually around 10-12 minutes.

For the bravas

Preheat the oven to 190°c. For this dish I like to cut my potatoes in a Parmentier style. To do this make sure you dice the potato into small squares of equal size. In a freezer bag, add in 4 tablespoons of olive oil, 5 cracked cloves of garlic, the smoked paprika and the red chillies. Mix well and then add the potatoes, ensuring they are all coated evenly. Remove from bag and place on a roasting tray in the oven until golden.

For the pea and onion fricassee

Peel and slice the onions as thinly as you can. Take a frying pan and add the chorizo oil followed by the butter. Add the onions and soften. Once the onions are ready, add the peas and warm through gently.

To plate

After letting the turkey rest for 10 minutes remove it from the bag and carve evenly. Lay the fricassee neatly in the centre of a large plate with the carved meat. Add a few of the Parmentier bravas around the edges and serve. Add in the chorizo crumb to finish. Remember you do not need to add everything, keep it neat and tidy. For the hungrier diner serve the rest of the meal in larger serving dishes so they can help themselves from the table.

Wild mushroom risotto

Serves 4

Refine this comfort food favourite and take it to the next level with some crispy sage leaves and a decadent drizzle of truffle oil.

INGREDIENTS

50g dried porcini

600ml vegetable/chicken stock

100ml mushroom stock

50g butter

2 tbsp olive oil

2 large shallots, chopped

200g arborio risotto rice

75ml dry vermouth

1 tbsp fresh thyme, chopped

½ tbsp fresh rosemary, chopped

½ tbsp fresh sage, chopped

2 large cloves garlic, peeled and minced

300g wild mushrooms, cleaned and chopped

3 tbsp Parmesan

Truffle oil

Sage leaves

Sea salt and white pepper

METHOD

For the crispy sage leaves

Take some time selecting the leaves you will be using. If you are cooking for four or six people make sure they are all the same size. It is little things like this that will take your home cooking to the next level. Have some kitchen paper ready and carefully but simply drop the leaves into some hot oil. Remove after around 20-30 seconds and drain immediately.

For the risotto

In a bowl add the dried porcini and top with 150ml of boiling water. Cover with cling film and set aside for 20 minutes.

Take two large saucepans and in one add the stock and heat gently. In the other add the butter and a splash of olive oil then soften the shallots. Next add the rice and coat evenly in the butter and oil, stirring continuously. Once coated add in the vermouth and cook off the alcohol.

Now over a bowl (you need to reserve the liquid) drain your dried porcini mushrooms though a J-cloth and a sieve. Chop them and set aside. Add the liquid to the rice, stirring all the time.

Now add in a ladle of stock and stir until the rice is drying out. Add the herbs, garlic and all of the chopped mushrooms. Continue to add stock a ladle at a time until you are left with a sticky creamy risotto that is just retaining a little bite. Now add the Parmesan, serve and garnish with crispy sage and a drizzle of truffle oil. Season to taste.

The Sea

Poached sea bass with brown butter and capers

Serves 4

This is a nice light fish dish that I tend to use on a tasting menu. It is served simply with brown butter and capers. The flavour and elegance of the dish speaks for itself.

INGREDIENTS

4 x 120g sea bass fillets

300ml milk

100ml water

2 bay leaves

Sea salt and white pepper

75g unsalted butter

30g capers

Fresh dill to garnish

METHOD

Score the fish in a criss-cross pattern and roll it gently, securing with a cocktail stick if necessary. If it is a long fillet you may need to halve it.

Add the milk, water, bay leaves and seasoning into a large frying pan. Gently poach the sea bass and simmer until the fish is just cooked through, which will be after around 3 to 4 minutes.

While your fish is poaching start melting the butter over a medium to high heat, gently swirling the pan to ensure the butter is cooking evenly. As the butter melts, it will start to foam. The colour will change to a nutty-brown. Once your butter is golden, take the pan off the heat and transfer the browned butter through a sieve or tea strainer to remove any sediment.

In the same pan gently fry the capers through until warm and just starting to crisp up.

To serve, simply add the fish to a wide rimmed bowl and top with the brown butter and capers. Add in a few dill fronds and serve immediately.

Devilled mackerel on toast

Serves 4

This oily fish offers a rich and distinctive flavour that is enhanced by a few choice spices. I've simply paired it with bitter sweet pickled cherries and a couple of carefully cut slices of Melba toast.

INGREDIENTS

4 mackerel, cleaned

Olive oil

25g butter, softened

1½ tsp cayenne

½ tsp paprika

1 tsp English mustard

1 tbsp crème fraîche

5-6 shakes Tabasco sauce

1 tbsp Worcester sauce

1½ tsp fine brown sugar

For the pickled cherries

500g black cherries

125ml red wine vinegar

300ml Barolo wine

6 tbsp white sugar

To finish

2 slices white bread, for the Melba toast

Fresh dill

METHOD

For the mackerel

Preheat the oven to 190°c. Rub then marinate the mackerel in all of the ingredients and leave for at least a couple of hours, but overnight if possible. When ready, rub the mackerel with a little olive oil and then roast skin side down for 15 minutes.

For the Melba toasts

These are simple to make and with a little extra effort can look visually stunning on this dish.

Take a rolling pin and some white bread with the crusts removed, place between two layers of cling film and roll out the bread until thin.

Next, carefully cut the bread into the desired shape, take extra care to make them uniform, remember it's those little details that make the difference!

On a baking tray, lay the bread between two pieces of baking paper, top with another tray and bake in the oven at 190°c until crisp.

For the pickled cherries

In a saucepan bring the vinegar and Barolo wine to the boil. Stir in the sugar and cook on a low heat for 5 minutes. This will allow just enough time to dissolve the sugar and slightly reduce the liquid. Now add in the cherries and cook for a further 2 minutes.

Remove the pan from the heat and leave the mixture to cool.

To plate

Serve the mackerel skin side up with the Melba toasts upright next to it and the cherries alongside. Finish with a sprig of dill.

Camarão frito with squid ink aioli

Serves 4

This is a tapas style dish made with delicious prawns, my panna gratta and a simple aioli with just a touch of squid ink.

INGREDIENTS

For the prawns
Olive oil

500g large prawns

2 cloves garlic, minced

1 tbsp parsley, chopped

½ lemon, juiced

2 tbsp panna gratta, see below

For the aioli
2 cloves garlic, minced

3 free-range egg yolks

½ lemon, juiced

Salt and freshly ground white pepper

150ml extra virgin olive oil

1 tsp squid ink

For the panna gratta
Stale ciabatta

Olive oil

Garlic clove

Sea salt

To garnish
Red chilli, thinly sliced

Micro herbs

Garlic, thinly sliced and fried

METHOD

For the panna gratta
Take a stale ciabatta and either chop or use a processor to break down into small bite size pieces and crumbs.

In a large frying pan add 3 tablespoons of oil and heat gently. With your knife crush a garlic clove just enough crack it open and fry off until just brown. At that point remove it from the oil and add in the breadcrumbs. Coat evenly and season with sea salt. Once they are starting to brown put them on a baking tray and toast gently in the oven for 10 minutes at 150°c until dry and crunchy.

For the prawns
Add the oil to a large frying pan then toss the prawns in the oil until they are starting to colour on all sides. This will take around 2 minutes. Then add in the garlic and stir well for 1 more minute. Add the parsley and lemon juice and serve with a little panna gratta while hot.

For the aioli
Blend the garlic, egg yolks, lemon juice and seasoning into a food processor. Blitz and once they are at a paste-like consistency, slowly and steadily pour the olive oil into the processor a little at a time, this will ensure you end up with a thick sauce. Now add the squid ink and stir well.

To plate
Arrange the prawns in a trio formation, top with panna gratta, micro herbs, flash fried garlic slices and add dots of the aioli topped with chilli slices as per the picture.

Grilled sardines with gremolata butter

Serves 4

Sardines have a brilliant, bold taste that stands up well against strong flavours like paprika, garlic and lemon. This dish combines all of the above with some fresh herbs to balance it out.

INGREDIENTS

For the butter

200g unsalted butter

1 lemon

1 tbsp flat leaf parsley, chopped

2 cloves garlic, minced

For the fish

1 tbsp smoked paprika

50g cornflour

12 sardines, cleaned

Micro basil

1 lemon, thinly sliced and dehydrated

METHOD

For the butter

Make sure your butter is at room temperature, and combine it with the juice and zest of the lemon, the parsley and garlic. Wrap this in baking paper and set aside.

For the fish

Mix the paprika and cornflour and gently dust the sardines. Place under a hot grill and cook for around 2 minutes on each side for a medium sized fish. If you have small sardines you may need to reduce this accordingly.

Take some of the butter and in a small frying pan start to brown it off over a medium heat. Add in some basil leaves to crisp up.

Pull the flesh from the fish and shape using round moulds. Plate alongside the lemon slices and garnish with the rest of the micro basil. Serve the sauce of the side.

Hot smoked mackerel and friends

Serves 4

You can smoke your own mackerel if you have the tools, it is easy enough but a shop bought one will be very good too, and will work perfectly well for this recipe. Having made this dish for a few critics I know your guests will enjoy it too!

INGREDIENTS

For the mash

120g butter

70g fresh horseradish, grated

100ml double cream

Salt and pepper

1kg rooster potatoes

For the bon-bons

150g hot smoked mackerel

150g dry mashed potato, cold

2 tbsp seasoned plain flour

2 eggs, beaten

100g fine breadcrumbs

Oil, for frying

For the mackerel fillets

4 mackerel fillets

Oil, for brushing

For the garnish

10 red grapes

10 green grapes

4 Charlotte potatoes, peeled and cooked

Chervil

1 grate fresh horseradish

METHOD

For the horseradish pomme purée

Add the butter, horseradish and cream to a saucepan. Season and heat through gently for 10 minutes. I like to leave this overnight to infuse and then re-heat and strain the bits of horseradish out before adding the potato.

Peel and then boil the potatoes until softened and pass through a potato ricer into a bowl. Slowly use a whisk to combine the horseradish infused warm cream and butter mixture, making sure you combine it gently without overworking it.

For the bon-bons

In a bowl flake the hot smoked mackerel and combine with the cold dry mashed potato. Shape these into evenly sized balls, and then roll in the flour, then the egg and then the breadcrumbs. It helps if you pop them in the freezer for 10 minutes then re-roll to perfect the shape.

Finally, deep fry at 190°c until golden brown and warmed throughout. This will take around 3 minutes. Drain on paper towels.

For the mackerel fillets

Brush with a little oil and pan fry these skin side down until golden in colour, turn in the pan and remove from the stove allowing the residual heat to finish the cooking.

For the garnish

I like to use my small baller on the grapes and the Charlotte potato to garnish this plate. Finally finish the dish with some chervil and a final grate of horseradish.

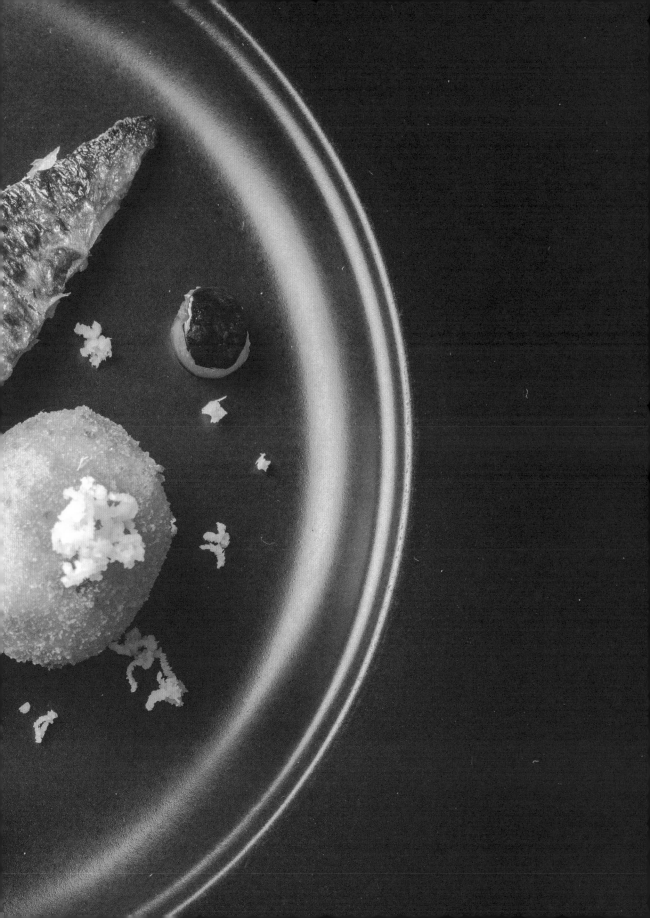

Halibut with petits pois a'la Française and pommes Anna

Serves 4

Halibut can often be quite expensive or difficult to get hold of, and although I have used it in this dish, you can easily substitute it for cod. It is best to make the pommes Anna the day before.

INGREDIENTS

For the pommes Anna

6 large red potatoes, peeled

250g butter

Salt and pepper

For the petits pois a'la Française

2 banana shallots, chopped

400g fresh or frozen peas

1 little gem lettuce, shredded

1 tbsp parsley

150ml chicken stock

100g pancetta lardons

Knob butter

1 tbsp crème fraîche

Sea salt and ground white pepper

For the fish

130g halibut fillet per person

Olive oil

Knob of butter

Sea salt and pepper

Pea shoots

METHOD

For the pommes Anna

Preheat the oven to 190°c. Using a mandoline if you have one, carefully slice the potatoes as thinly as possible, around 5mm thick.

In a saucepan, gently melt all of the butter. Use a brush to coat the bottom of a 25cm x 5cm roasting tray with 1½ tablespoons of the melted butter. Carefully cut out a square of greaseproof paper large enough to cover the bottom and the sides of the dish. Brush again with butter and start to layer the potato in an overlapped style along the dish. Brush again with melted butter and season well. Repeat until your dish is almost full and then pour over any remaining butter. Bake until the potatoes are fork-tender, usually after around 1 hour. Leave to cool for 30 minutes to let the butter firm up a little. Now you need to press the potato. I use an old plate and some tins from the cupboard to weight it down. Place in the fridge overnight to set and then the next day cut into the style you would like and heat through in the oven before serving.

For the petits pois a'la Française

I once got told that these were "the best peas ever" which was quite a compliment! They are a simple accompaniment to lots of dishes and a great side order to have up your sleeve. There are some simple things that make these great; prepare everything in advance, have the shallots finely chopped, the peas defrosted (if using frozen) and the lettuce and parsley chopped. Also, have the chicken stock warm and ready.

In a frying pan sauté the pancetta until golden. Remove it from the pan and soften the shallots in the remaining fat. Next add a knob of butter and the peas, parsley and lettuce. The key here is to move fast, they don't really need any cooking at all, so 30 seconds to warm through is plenty. Stir in the crème fraîche and season.

For the fish

Remove the skin from the fish and rub with a little olive oil. Season and place into a hot frying pan until golden. Add a knob of butter and baste the fish using a spoon. Use a fish slice to gently turn the fish and cook until firm and golden but still white-ish in the middle. It's important to let the fish rest a little, around a minute or so. Garnish with pea shoots.

Roast hake with fennel hollandaise

Serves 4

Hake is a versatile fish that absorbs a lot of flavour in its flaky flesh, making it perfect for this buttery hollandaise sauce and aromatic fennel.

INGREDIENTS

For the fennel hollandaise
2 fennel bulbs, with leafy green fronds
50g butter
4 large free-range egg yolks
¼ lemon, juice only
½ tbsp white wine vinegar

For the fish
4 x 140g hake fillets
250g cold unsalted butter, diced
Sea salt and white pepper
Lumpfish caviar

METHOD

For the hollandaise
Very finely chop the green fennel fronds and set aside.
In a saucepan start to gently melt the butter. Set a clear glass bowl on a tea towel to stop it moving, add in the egg yolks and whisk until creamy. Add in the lemon juice and vinegar and continue to whisk into a creamy thick paste. Now here is where you must be patient, very slowly start to pour in the melted butter, whisking continually until the sauce thickens. Now add in the fennel fronds and combine well.

For the fish
Preheat the oven to 180°c. Gently brush the hake fillets with melted butter and season with white pepper and just a little sea salt. Place them into an oven tray, and cook for about 8-10 minutes, until the flesh has turned opaque and flaky.

For the fennel
I like to slice my fennel thinly and then sauté it off in butter until soft and just starting to colour.
Once finished top the fish with the lumpfish caviar and serve.

Roasted cod
with sweet leeks and pickled fennel

Serves 4

This is a dish that has grown with me since my time in Sweden during MasterChef. I've developed it with a few additions and some new surprises that will impress anyone you have over for dinner.

INGREDIENTS

For the pickled fennel

1 fennel bulb, thinly sliced (reserve the herb tops for garnish)

50ml Attika (Swedish pickling vinegar)

100g sugar

150ml water

For the cod

130g cod fillet per person

Melted butter, for brushing

For the sweet leeks

4 leeks

150g butter

100g golden sugar

2 tbsp fresh parsley, chopped

For the burnt leek

1 leek

For the crispy chicken skin

100g white sugar

2 chicken breast skins

Sea salt

White pepper

METHOD

For the pickled fennel

To make my pickled fennel I use Attika Swedish Pickling Vinegar and the Swedish 3-2-1 pickling formula (available online).

Add the fennel to a saucepan containing the Attika, sugar and water and bring to the boil. Remove from the heat and place into sterilised jars. This will keep in the fridge for up to 3 months, although it can be used straight away if required.

For the cod

Preheat the oven to 190°c.

On a baking tray brush the cod with melted butter and season well. Bake in the oven for around 8 minutes. I aim to have mine out of there when the fish reaches 54°c in the centre.

For the sweet leeks

Thinly slice the leeks, wash them and then add them to a large saucepan. Soften in the butter, add in the golden sugar and continue to stir. Once soft and sweet remove them from the heat and leave them to cool slightly before adding in the parsley.

For the burnt leek

Preheat the oven to 190°c.

Slice the leek into thin long strips and lay on a baking tray between two pieces of baking paper. Top with another tray and bake until crisp and golden.

For the crispy chicken skin

This is the hidden gem of the dish, offering up a great boost of flavour and an extra element of texture. Remove the skin from two chicken breasts and lay the skin on a baking tray between two pieces of baking paper after brushing with a little oil and seasoning with sea salt. Top with another tray and bake in the oven until crisp and golden.

Spicy fish goujons
with aioli and Parmentier potatoes

Serves 4

This is my twist on a classic fish and chips dinner. I've added subtle spices like cayenne and saffron to really bring it alive.

INGREDIENTS

For the fish

400g filleted red mullet, sliced

2 tbsp cayenne pepper

150ml milk, seasoned with white pepper and sea salt

4 tbsp cornflour

Vegetable oil, for frying

For the potato

1 large Maris Piper potato

Extra virgin olive oil

For the aioli

2 cloves garlic, minced

3 free-range egg yolks

½ lemon, juice only

A small pinch of saffron

Salt and freshly ground white pepper

150ml extra virgin olive oil

Micro coriander, to garnish

METHOD

For the fish

Once the fish has been sliced into strips, toss in the cayenne pepper until evenly coated. Next brush with the milk and then carefully dust on all sides with the cornflour. I like to use a tea strainer to do this. Next, in batches, fry them in hot oil for around 2 minutes.

For the potato

Preheat the oven to 200°c. Slice the potato into perfect 1cm square dice. If you take that extra bit of care here then your dish will take on a really professional look. Toss the diced potato in some extra virgin olive oil and roast in the oven for 20 minutes or until golden on all sides.

For the aioli

Blend the garlic, egg yolks, lemon juice, saffron and seasoning in a food processor. Once they are at a paste-like consistency, slowly and steadily pour the olive oil into the processor a little at a time. This will ensure you end up with a thick yellow sauce with flecks of saffron running through it.

Marvellous
Meat

Balmoral chicken, turnips, swede and potato

Serves 4

This root vegetable and chicken dish looks fantastic whilst still retaining those hearty winter warming flavours.

INGREDIENTS

4 chicken breasts, skin removed

12 slices Parma ham

For the filling

1 small haggis

For the thyme and whiskey chicken jus

Knob butter

2 shallots, chopped

3 sprigs thyme

2 shots whiskey

2 pints chicken stock

For the potato

1 jar goose fat

3 large Désirée potatoes

For the swede purée

400ml carrot juice

3 sprigs thyme

150g swede, peeled and chopped

75g carrot, peeled and chopped

20g butter

For the turnips

8 baby turnips

Red amaranth, to garnish

Chicken skin (optional)

METHOD

For the chicken ballotine

Remove the haggis from its casing and crumble it using a fork for your filling. Butterfly the chicken breast on a chopping board. Place a sheet of cling film on a clean board and place the Parma ham slices on top with no gaps. Place the butterflied breast on top. Take the filling and spoon it in a line down the centre of the chicken. Using the cling film, roll the chicken breast up into a sausage shape, then twist the cling film at both ends to secure it (like wrapping up a sweet).

Place the cling film wrapped chicken in a pan of boiling water. Simmer for 20 minutes, resting a ladle on the chicken ballotine to hold it under the water if it starts to float. Remove the ballotine using a slotted spoon and allow to cool for a few moments. Remove the cling film.

For the thyme and whiskey chicken jus

Melt the butter in a medium saucepan and gently sauté the shallots. Once softened add the thyme and cook for a further minute, then add the whiskey and cook off the alcohol. Add the chicken stock and reduce by three quarters. This will only leave you a little jus but it will pack an amazing flavour punch so you won't need too much of it. Pass through a sieve to remove the shallots and thyme before serving.

For the potato

Preheat the oven to 190°c. Place the goose fat in a roasting tray and heat through. Peel the potato, and taking extra care use a round cutter to make a 4cm tall 3cm in diameter cut of potato. Ensure they are all uniform in size and shape. Season and place the potato in the hot fat and roast until golden for 45 minutes or until cooked through.

For the swede purée and turnips

In a saucepan add the carrot juice and thyme. Season and boil the swede and carrot for 20 minutes until tender. Remove the thyme and drain, retaining some of the liquor in case you need to loosen the purée. Transfer to a food processor, add the butter, season well, then blitz to a purée. I add my purée to a squeezy bottle to make plating neater.

Clean the turnips leaving the leaf stalk intact on four of them and the root intact on the other four – this will give your guests one of each. Level the alternate ends and then gently boil for around 80 minutes until tender.

After resting for 5 minutes carefully slice the ballotine on an angle and use the squeezy bottle to add your purée to the plate. Finish with the jus and a scattering of red amaranth.

Gyros pork with flat breads and oregano tzatziki

Serves 4

This is my take on a traditional Greek dish, combining succulent tenderloin pork with homemade flat bread and cooling creamy tzatziki. It's a great dish to try out your plating skills as it perfectly lends itself to a symmetrical trio formation.

INGREDIENTS

For the gyros pork

1 pork tenderloin

50g butter

3 cloves garlic, chopped

2 red onions, sliced

4 tbsp extra virgin olive oil

1 tbsp red wine vinegar

1 tbsp fresh oregano, chopped

1 tbsp fresh thyme

1 tbsp rosemary, chopped

1 tbsp honey

For the flat bread

300g self-raising flour

1 tsp baking powder

300g natural yoghurt

½ tsp sea salt

For the oregano tzatziki

50ml extra virgin olive oil

2 tbsp fresh oregano, chopped

2 cloves garlic, minced

1 cucumber, peeled and de-seeded

500g natural yoghurt

To garnish

1 chilli, thinly sliced

Micro herbs

METHOD

For the pork

If you have one, set your sous vide machine to 61°c and add the pork, along with all the other ingredients in a sealed bag for 3 hours. If you don't have a sous vide, you can get similar results by covering the pork in tin foil and then sitting it on a wire rack above a tray filled with all the other ingredients in the oven on 160°c for 1.5 hours. Once cooked, drain and retain all of the liquor ingredients and rest the pork for 10 minutes.

Add all of the liquor ingredients to a processor and blitz into a paste. Carefully and neatly slice the pork into 1.5cm medallions and then coat in the paste.

When ready to serve, bring a large frying pan to a high heat and fry on one side for 1 minute until golden. Take care not to overcook the pork.

For the flat bread

Simply mix all of the flat bread ingredients together in a bowl. Cover with cling film and set aside to rest for 20 minutes. Using lightly floured hands, roll into evenly sized balls, flatten and then toast in a dry frying pan until golden on both sides. Use a cutter to refine the shape of the bread to elevate the style of your dish.

For the oregano tzatziki

In a food processor add the olive oil, oregano and garlic and blend.

In a large bowl grate the peeled and de-seeded cucumber and season with salt. Set it aside for 10 minutes so the moisture comes out of the cucumber. Drain this off and then to really dry out the remaining grated cucumber, wrap it in a towel and squeeze until it is dry. Next in a bowl, add the cucumber, the contents of your processor, the yogurt and combine well.

To plate

Arrange the pork in the middle of the plate in a trio formation, with the flat bread slices between each slice along with dots of the tzatziki. Garnish with the chilli slices and micro herbs.

Chargrilled lamb cutlets with feta and aubergine

Serves 4

This dish shows that even the simplest of marinades can make all of the difference. It doesn't take too long to make at all so it's perfect if you're in a bit of a hurry but still want to cook up something special.

INGREDIENTS

For the lamb

300g natural yoghurt

50ml olive oil

Large bunch fresh oregano, chopped

Salt and pepper, to season

12 lamb cutlets

For the aubergines

8 baby aubergines

Olive oil, for brushing

2 small red onions, peeled and halved

1 red chilli

50g black olives

To garnish

150g feta

METHOD

For the lamb

In a food processor, blitz the yoghurt, olive oil and oregano and season well. Save a third of this for the garnish and then add the cutlets to a bowl and coat well in the remaining marinade.

Cook on a griddle until charred and nicely cooked, and then set aside to rest.

For the aubergines

Brush the aubergines with a little oil and season, then use the griddle pan to char and cook them through.

Add some foil in a frying pan and gently burn the red onion.

Finely slice the chilli and olives and use these along with some oregano and the remaining yoghurt to garnish your plate.

Finally crumble the feta over.

Chimichurri ribeye with refried bean fritters

Serves 4

Originating in Argentina, the fragrant and flavoursome chimichurri is made for garnishing meat dishes like this one. Keep the refried bean fritters looking nice and neat by using a mould and popping them in the freezer to set slightly.

INGREDIENTS

For the chimichurri

Fresh parsley, large bunch

2 tbsp fresh oregano

2 garlic clove, minced

1 shallot, chopped

½ tsp chilli flakes

3 tbsp olive oil

1 lime, juice

1 tsp red wine vinegar

For the ribeye steaks

4 x 180g ribeye steaks

Olive oil and a pinch of sea salt

Knob of butter

For the refried bean fritters

1 red onion, finely chopped

2 garlic cloves, minced

1 tsp ground coriander

2 tsp smoked paprika

400g tin pinto or kidney beans, rinsed

1 tbsp plain flour

1 egg

4 tbsp breadcrumbs

To garnish

1 red chilli, thinly sliced

Micro coriander

50g sour cream (optional)

METHOD

For the chimichurri

Simply add all of the ingredients to a food processor and blitz until you have a vibrant green paste. You'll need a small amount to add to the steaks just at the end of cooking, and then the rest to serve as a garnish to your dish.

For the ribeye steaks

I like to sous vide steak as it keeps the flavours packed in, making it both juicy and tender. For a 180g steak medium rare, it will take 1 hour at 53°c. After 60 minutes remove the steak and dry on a J-cloth. Rub with a little olive oil and season with sea salt, and then finish in a hot pan with butter, adding a little of the chimichurri just at the end of cooking.

Alternatively, if you don't have a sous vide, you can simply pan fry to your liking, adding the chimichurri right at the end.

You should always set the steak aside to rest for 5 minutes before carving.

For the refried bean fritters

In a large frying pan gently soften and just start to brown the onion and garlic. Add the coriander and smoked paprika and cook for a further minute.

Add ¾ of the rinsed and drained beans into a mixing bowl and use a fork or a potato masher to crush into a chunky paste. In a food processor blitz the remaining beans and then combine them together, along with the flour, egg and breadcrumbs.

Once cool carefully shape the mixture into balls around 2cm across. For this recipe I use a spherical mould to get the right shape. Add the mould to the freezer to harden slightly, which will keep the shape when you take them out. Gently fry the beans at 190°c until golden.

To plate

Carefully slice the steak and delicately place the fritters on the plate, add some extra chimichurri and top with small slices of chilli, coriander and dots of sour cream.

Pig cheeks with anise, black pudding and celeriac

Serves 4

Pig cheeks are a great underused cut of pork, they are best cooked low and slow. Here I'm using a sous vide method as I find this gives the best results. No sous vide? Don't worry you can get a great end product in the oven at 130°c for 5 hours.

INGREDIENTS

For the pig cheeks

4 pig cheeks

1 star anise

1 stick celery, chopped

1 onion, chopped

1 carrot, chopped

300ml chicken stock

For the black pudding

1 black pudding

1 tsp vegetable oil

For the celeriac

2 celeriac

Oil, for brushing

100ml double cream

Sea salt and white pepper

30g butter

Micro fennel, to garnish

METHOD

For the pig cheeks

Add a little olive oil to a large frying pan, crank up the heat and quickly brown the pig cheeks on both sides. Set them aside to rest and in the same pan add in the star anise, celery, onion and carrot. Brown gently and then add the chicken stock and reduce by half. Set aside to cool, and then add everything into a bag and place in the sous vide at 80°c for 8 hours. Alternatively, use the slow cook method above.

Remove, drain and set aside to rest. Sieve the liquor and reduce until thickened in a saucepan.

For the black pudding

Remove the skin from the black pudding and in a food processor blitz into a crumb, then add a little oil into a frying pan and toast the pudding crumble until it's just crunchy.

For the celeriac

Peel the celeriac and taking extra care cut out 8 cubes that are exactly 1.5cm square. Brush with a little oil and roast in the oven for 20 minutes until soft and just golden.

For the celeriac purée

Add 500g of small diced celeriac to a saucepan with the double cream. Cook over a low heat until it is soft. Season heavily with salt and white pepper and then add into a food processor with the butter and blitz until smooth and creamy.

Duck and dauphinoise
with caramelised chicory

Serves 4

To take this dish to the next level add my caramelised chicory (page 177) and crispy sage (page 179) to garnish. It is best to make the dauphinoise the day before so they have time to set overnight.

INGREDIENTS

For the dauphinoise

1kg Désirée potatoes

50g butter

Salt and pepper

For the duck

4 duck breasts

For the jus

Knob of butter

1 shallot

1 star anise

500ml chicken stock

3 cloves garlic, minced

350ml double cream

To garnish

2 chicories

12 sage leaves

METHOD

For the dauphinoise

Preheat your oven to 160°c.

Very carefully using a mandoline, slice the potatoes as thinly as possible, around 5mm thick or thinner.

In a saucepan gently melt the butter and use it to coat the bottom of a 25cm wide 5cm deep roasting tray with a brush. Carefully cut out a square of greaseproof paper large enough to cover the bottom and the sides of the dish, brush again with butter and start to layer the potato in an overlapped style along the dish. Season each layer well with salt and pepper. Repeat until the dish is almost full to the top.

Use the back of a knife to mince the garlic into a smooth paste and stir into the cream. Pour over the potatoes and bake until they are tender, usually after around 1 hour and 15 minutes.

Remove from the oven and leave to cool for 30 minutes. To press the potatoes use a plate to weigh them down. Place the dauphinoise in the fridge overnight to set and then the next day you can cut in to the shape you would like, before heating through in the oven to serve.

For the duck

In a cold dry pan place the duck skin side down over a medium heat. Do not add any oil as the skin has a high fat content and is incredibly tasty once crisp. Allow the pan to warm gently and slowly render the fat out until it is golden and crispy in colour. This will usually take around 7 minutes. Once golden, season with sea salt then turn and brown on the other side for a couple of minutes. Remove and rest skin side up on a wire rack over a tray before carving.

For the jus

In a saucepan gently melt a little butter over a medium heat and add the shallot and star anise. Cook for two minutes until softened then add the chicken stock and turn up the heat and boil rapidly until the liquid has reduced by half. Add in the juices from your now rested duck before using a sieve to remove the shallots and the anise.

Once you've plated the dish, drizzle a spoonful of jus around the duck.

Pigeon, celeriac and vichy heritage carrots

Serves 4

This dish has been developed from my main course in the final of MasterChef, I hope you have as much fun replicating it as I had inventing it.

INGREDIENTS

For the pigeon

4 pigeon breasts

Smoked sea salt and a knob of butter

For the celeriac purée

500g celeriac, diced

150ml double cream

Sea salt and freshly ground white pepper

30g butter

For the carrots

12 vichy heritage carrots, various colours

Sprig fresh thyme

200ml carrot juice

1 tbsp caster sugar

20ml white wine vinegar

For the pommes Parisienne

2 large Maris Piper potatoes, peeled

Oil, for deep frying and smoked sea salt

Red wine reduction

50g butter

1 shallot, finely chopped

Sprig thyme

100ml red wine

50ml chicken stock

Micro celery, to garnish

METHOD

For the pigeon

Place a frying pan over a medium to high heat and add a little olive oil. Season both sides of the pigeon breasts with salt then add to the pan and cook until golden, for around 3 minutes. Turn the breasts, add a knob of butter and baste the meat for another 2-3 minutes. Remove the breasts from the pan and leave to rest for approximately 5 minutes before carving into two even pieces.

For the celeriac purée

Add the celeriac to a saucepan with the double cream and cook over a low heat until it is soft. Season heavily with salt and white pepper and then add into a food processor with the butter and blitz until smooth and creamy.

For the carrots

Clean the carrots taking extra care around the stalks. Add them to a frying pan with the thyme, carrot juice, sugar and vinegar and cook until soft.

For the pommes Parisienne

Take a mini melon baller, and shape around 6-8 balls of potato per person. Gently deep fry these at 190°c and then season in smoked sea salt.

For the red wine reduction

In a saucepan gently melt the butter over a medium heat and add the shallot and thyme and cook for two minutes until softened. Next add the red wine and the chicken stock and turn up the heat. Boil rapidly until the liquid has reduced by half, sieve to remove the shallots and the thyme and add a spoonful to your finished dish.

Turkey and tarragon Parma with Parmentier potatoes

Serves 4

Serve this delicious dish with my classic tomato sauce recipe and some tarragon crisps (page 179).

INGREDIENTS

For the turkey

2 mozzarella balls

1 tbsp fresh tarragon

100g sundried tomatoes

100g Parmesan, grated

75g butter, soft

4 turkey breast steaks

12 slices Parma ham

For the Parmentier potato

1 large Maris Piper potato

Extra virgin olive oil

Sea salt and white pepper

For the tomato sauce

1 tbsp olive oil

2 cloves garlic, crushed into a paste

2 shallots, finely diced

3 tsp fresh oregano

1 tbsp tomato purée

10 ripe cherry tomatoes, quartered

1 litre passata

1 tin chopped tomatoes

70g fresh basil, chopped

Sea salt and white pepper

METHOD

For the turkey and tarragon Parma

Take the mozzarella, tarragon and sundried tomatoes and finely chop them. In a bowl combine with the Parmesan and butter and season well.

Next, lay the turkey between two sheets of cling film and gently flatten with a rolling pin, then set aside. Lay out a long length of cling film, fold it across itself to double it up and then layer 3 slices of Parma ham on it. Top this with the turkey, and at one end add in the cheese and tomato mixture. Then roll the turkey into a sausage, securing with a knot at either end.

In a saucepan poach this for 15 minutes and then set aside to rest for 5 minutes. Remove from the cling film and then brown in a frying pan before removing the ends and then neatly slicing.

For the Parmentier potato

Preheat the oven to 200°c.

Cut the potato into perfect 1cm square dice, as always take extra care here for that professional look. Toss the diced potato in some extra virgin olive oil, sea salt and white pepper and roast in the oven for 20 minutes or until golden on all sides.

For the tomato sauce

In a large saucepan gently heat the olive oil and then add in the garlic paste. Stir gently for around 20 seconds, then add in the shallots and soften gently for a couple of minutes.

Once the shallots are softened add in the oregano and tomato purée and cook for another minute stirring frequently. Next add the quartered cherry tomatoes, the passata and the tin of chopped tomatoes. Cook the sauce gently for 15 minutes, stir in the chopped basil and cook for another 20 seconds. Season.

To plate

Garnish with tarragon crisps and swoosh of the tomato sauce.

Shredded pork ribs with balsamic and pomegranate cabbage

Serves 4

I like to sous vide these ribs for 18 hours at 82°c. However if you don't have the equipment you can cover them in foil, add 200ml water to a roasting tray and cook them in the oven at 150°c for 4 hours.

INGREDIENTS

For the ribs
750g pork ribs
3 tsp olive oil

For the cabbage
1 shallot, finely chopped
3 tsp oil
400g shredded red cabbage
100ml pomegranate juice
Pinch sea salt
50ml Belazu balsamic vinegar

For the leek
1 leek

To garnish
Micro broccoli (herb)
Pomegranate seeds

METHOD

For the ribs
Cook the pork ribs using either of the methods above, according to the equipment you have. Once cooked use a fork to shred the meat from the bones and then in a frying pan add a little oil to crisp it up a little.

For the cabbage
Add the shallot and a little oil to a saucepan and sauté gently. Add the cabbage and stir well, before adding the pomegranate juice and a little sea salt. Cover with a lid and cook until the liquid has almost vanished and the cabbage is thick and sticky. Now add the balsamic and stir well until you have a nice deep purple sticky and shiny cabbage.

For the leek
Take the white end of the leek and slice 1.5cm rounds, add them into a dry frying pan and blacken to really emphasise the rings of the leek.

To plate
Combine the cabbage, pork and a handful of pomegranate seeds, then plate the dish using a chef's ring with the micro herbs on top and the burnt leek around the cabbage.

Vegetarian

Simply curried cauliflower

Serves 4

This recipe shows just how versatile one ingredient can be. It's also a great example of how you can approach plating a dish with a bit of finesse. My advice is to practise swiping and dotting the sauce before presenting your final dish.

INGREDIENTS

For the curried cauliflower purée

½ tsp coriander seeds, whole

½ tsp cumin seeds, whole

1 tbsp mild curry powder

½ large cauliflower

1 garlic clove, minced

25g butter

150ml double cream

1 pinch saffron

For the cauliflower crisp

4 thin slices cauliflower

25ml olive oil

Sea salt

For the roasted cauliflower

¼ large cauliflower

For the cauliflower couscous

¼ large cauliflower

Micro coriander

METHOD

For the curried cauliflower purée

In a large saucepan gently toast the coriander and cumin seeds to release their flavours. This will only take a couple of minutes. Place them into a pestle and mortar and crush into a powder. Add in the curry powder and mix well.

Take the half of cauliflower and cut it into chunks. Add to a saucepan with the garlic, butter, cream, half of the spices, and the saffron. Cook gently until softened and then blitz in a food processor until smooth.

For the cauliflower crisp

Preheat the oven to 190°c.

Use a sharp knife and as thinly as possible shave a thin sliver of cauliflower for each person. Take a baking tray, lay the cauliflower between two pieces of baking paper, brush it with a little oil and season with sea salt. Top with another tray and bake in the oven until crisp and golden.

For the roasted cauliflower

Turn the oven up to 200°c.

Take the quarter of cauliflower, cut into even-sized chunks and add to a bowl with the rest of the spices and olive oil. Mix well and roast in the oven for 15 minutes.

For the cauliflower couscous

Take the rest of the cauliflower and blitz in a food processor until it has a couscous style texture. Use this to finish your dish with a touch of micro coriander.

Goat's cheese bon-bons with chutney, greens and beets

Serves 4

The combination of goat's cheese and beetroot is timeless. Here's my take on the classic, which incorporates crispy bon-bons, freshly sliced beetroot, zingy chutney and buttery spinach.

INGREDIENTS

For the chutney

300g beetroot, chopped

Olive oil

1 red onion, grated

1 red chilli, chopped

175ml red wine vinegar

½ tsp sea salt

Pinch white pepper

75g brown sugar

For the bon-bons

125g soft goat's cheese

2 eggs, beaten

2 tbsp plain flour

2 tbsp breadcrumbs

Vegetable oil, for deep frying

For the spinach

50g butter

1 clove black garlic, minced

160g spinach

Fresh nutmeg

Beetroot leaves

Golden beetroot

METHOD

For the chutney

Preheat the oven to 190°c. Wearing gloves peel and chop the beetroot, drizzle with a little olive oil and then roast in the oven until softened. Remove and leave to cool. In a frying pan add olive oil followed by the onion and soften. Next add in the chilli and cook for 2 minutes stirring continuously. Now add the roasted beetroot and onion to a food processor and pulse. Return to the frying pan and add the red wine vinegar, salt, pepper and sugar and bring to the boil for 20 minutes, stirring frequently.

For the bon-bons

Separate the goat's cheese into roughly 15g portions and roll into balls. Take your time and make sure that they are all identical. Next you need to pane the cheese. To do this, first of all dip it in the flour and then in the egg, followed by the breadcrumbs. Place them into the freezer to just firm up for 5 minutes and then remove and reshape if necessary. Deep fry them at 190°c until golden.

For the spinach

In a large saucepan, heat the butter and garlic. Next add in the washed spinach and cover for 30 seconds. Stir and add 3 grates of fresh nutmeg then cover again for 30 seconds. Plate this using a 2cm round chef's ring to shape it.

Drop the beetroot leaves into a large pan of boiling water for 10 seconds and then immediately refresh in ice cold water. Next take the golden beetroot and slice into thin round discs. Finish the plate with dots of the chutney and the blanched beetroot leaves, followed by the crispy cheese bon-bons.

Brassica gratin

Serves 4

This is my more sophisticated approach to a cheesy vegetable dish, showcasing the beautiful shape of Romanesco broccoli. I use just a touch of the sauce to keep it looking fresh and green, whilst still retaining a nice creamy flavour. You can always put extra cheese sauce on the table for those who want to add more.

INGREDIENTS

For the cheese sauce
40g butter

40g flour

290ml milk

100g cheddar cheese

For the gratin
1 Romanesco broccoli

2 green broccoli stalks, with leaves

1 garlic clove, minced

Sea salt and white pepper

METHOD

For the cheese sauce
In a medium sized saucepan dissolve the butter and add in the flour, stirring until the mixture forms a paste. Cook this for a minimum of 2 minutes to cook out the flour. Warm the milk gently in a small saucepan then slowly, little by little, add the milk to the other mixture. Stir until smooth. Now add the cheddar cheese and allow to melt gently.

For the gratin
Preheat the oven to 210°c.

Remove the stalks from the broccoli, peel and then slice thinly, using a mandoline if you have one. Use a circular cutter to make sure that each slice is exactly the same size.

In a roasting tray lay out half of the broccoli stems and carefully cover with some of the cheese sauce, bake in the oven until golden and soft, around 8 minutes. If you need to add more colour you can always pop them under the grill.

Take the Romanesco and carefully click off the little triangular florets. Boil these until tender in salted water and then immediately refresh in some ice water. Repeat this with the remaining circular stems and leaves.

To plate
Next, plate delicately with the leaves and dots of the cheese sauce.

Minted pea falafel with carrot, onion and cucumber salad

Serves 4

Petits pois and fresh herbs like mint and parsley add a lovely vibrancy to this falafel dish. You can be quite elegant with the plating of the salad by using a speed peeler.

INGREDIENTS

For the falafel

300g frozen petits pois, thawed

200g chickpeas, drained

3 tbsp flour

2 garlic cloves, crushed

1 tsp ground cumin

1 tsp cayenne pepper

½ tsp ground coriander

2 tbsp smooth peanut butter

50g fresh parsley, chopped

50g fresh mint, chopped

1 lemon, zest and juice

Oil, for deep frying

For the garnish

1 large cucumber

Sea salt

1 bunch large heritage carrots, various colours

Mint leaves

Micro coriander

Spring onions (optional)

For the dressing

Carrot tops

300g natural yoghurt

Sea salt and white pepper

METHOD

For the falafel

In a food processor, combine all of the ingredients into a smooth paste. Leave to chill in the fridge and then roll into even sized spheres that are around 25g each. Deep fry at 190°c until golden.

For the garnish

Take half of the cucumber and using a speed peeler make long ribbons around 4-5 millimetres thick. Take care not to include any of the seeds, only the flesh. Next cut them into even sized rectangles and lay them on a baking tray. Season with a good amount of sea salt and then place in the freezer for 30 minutes.

Remove the cucumber and allow to defrost, you'll notice the change in consistency; you can now roll these into tubes ready to fill with your dressing.

Using a speed peeler, make long ribbons of carrot and set aside ready to garnish.

For the dressing

Blend half of the yoghurt in a food processor with some of the carrot tops. Season the other half of the yoghurt with sea salt and white pepper and add both of them to different piping bags.

To plate

Make some crispy mint leaves (see page 179) and delicately plate the dish taking extra care when you pipe the cucumber with the sauces. Finish the plate with a flourish of coriander and spring onions if you are using them.

Gruyère squash with chilli

Serves 4

The peculiar shape of pattypan squash adds an interesting visual element to this dish, as does the height of the courgette flower. Keep it looking neat by piping dots of the cheese sauce around the vegetables; you can always put an extra serving dish of the sauce on the table for those who want more.

INGREDIENTS

For the cheese sauce
40g butter
40g flour
290ml milk
100g Gruyère cheese

For the Gruyère crisp
70g Gruyère cheese, grated

For the squash
4 pattypan squash
50ml olive oil
Sea salt
1 garlic clove, minced
1 spring rosemary
1 red chilli, thinly sliced
4 courgette flowers

rosemary sprig

METHOD

For the cheese sauce
In a medium sized saucepan dissolve the butter and add in the flour, stirring until the mixture forms a paste. Cook this for a minimum of 2 minutes to cook out the flour. Heat the milk in a small saucepan taking care that it doesn't boil over. Carefully and slowly, a little at a time, add in the milk. Stir until the mixture is smooth. Add in 100g of the Gruyère cheese and allow to melt gently.

For the Gruyère crisp
Preheat the oven to 190°c. On a non-stick baking tray use a chefs ring to make 8cm rounds of the grated Gruyère cheese. Put them in the oven for a couple of minutes. Keep a close eye on them, they won't take long. Remove from the oven and allow to cool; you can cut out a neater shape once almost cooled with a slightly smaller cutter.

For the squash
Slice the squash into quarters, and in a roasting tray toss in some olive oil, sea salt, garlic and rosemary. Bake in the oven until sticky and golden, depending on the size of your squash this will usually take around 25 minutes at 190°c.

For the crispy rosemary
Have some kitchen paper ready and carefully but simply drop the leaves into some hot oil. Remove after around 20-30 seconds and drain immediately.

To plate
To finish, garnish the plate with dots of the cheese sauce, the Gruyère crisp, some thinly sliced red chilli, crispy rosemary and finally the courgette flower.

Za'atar aubergine with coconut cream and tabbouleh

Serves 4

The lightness of the tabbouleh and creamy coconut flavour cuts through the spicy aubergine brilliantly on this dish. You can get za'atar spice mix from most good supermarkets and it's handy to have in your cupboards for quick marinades like this one.

INGREDIENTS

For the tabbouleh

30g bulgur wheat

2 tomatoes

1 large bunch fresh flat leaf parsley, chopped

2 tbsp fresh mint leaves, chopped

1 small red onion, finely diced

1 lemon, juice and zest

Extra virgin olive oil

Sea salt and black pepper

For the aubergines

1 tbsp za'atar spice mix

30ml extra virgin olive oil

8 baby aubergines

For the sauce

1 tin/carton coconut cream

Micro herbs, to garnish

METHOD

For the tabbouleh

First of all, place the bulgur wheat into a small bowl and cover with 60ml of boiling water. Mix it well then cover with some cling film and leave it to absorb the water for 20 minutes.

Place the tomatoes into some boiling water for 20 seconds, prick with a knife and then gently peel the skin off and quarter them, discard the seeds and dice into evenly sized pieces.

Add the parsley, mint and onion to the tomatoes, then mix well with 3 tablespoons of lemon juice and all of the zest.

Gently use a fork to fluff the bulgur wheat until the grains are separated. Combine with the herbs, onion and tomatoes, dress with olive oil and season to taste.

For the aubergines

Preheat the oven to 200°c. Combine the za'atar with 30ml of olive oil. Halve the aubergines and coat them evenly in the paste you have made. Lay them face down on a baking tray and roast in the oven until tender. Brush them again midway through, after around 5-6 minutes.

For the coconut cream

This is really easy and a great addition to this dish, all you need is a small piping bag and a tin or carton of coconut cream. Simply separate the thick cream and add it into the piping bag, seal it and use this as a sauce to dot around the aubergines.

To plate

Using a chef's ring, pile the tabbouleh neatly in the centre of the plate and arrange the aubergines on top. Garnish with micro herbs.

Peppercorn wild mushrooms on toast

Serves 4

Sometimes you just can't beat mushrooms on toast. My version with fresh woody herbs and crushed peppercorns will add that extra kick to an old favourite.

INGREDIENTS

For the toast

25g butter

1 tsp fresh sage

1 tsp fresh thyme

1 tsp fresh rosemary

1 clove garlic, minced

1 ciabatta loaf

For the mushrooms

400g wild mushrooms, cleaned

25g butter

10 green peppercorns, crushed

75ml Worcestershire sauce

4 tbsp crème fraîche

METHOD

For the toast

Add the butter to a large frying pan. Sauté the herbs and garlic for 1 minute. Leave the butter in the pan but remove the herbs and set aside. Next slice the ciabatta and neatly shape it using cutters before frying off on both sides in the now flavoured butter. Set the toast aside on a rack.

For the mushrooms

Use a paintbrush to clean the mushrooms, and then add the butter to the frying pan. Add the mushrooms and brown. Once they are golden add the sautéed herbs and stir well. Next add the peppercorns, making sure that you have crushed them quite fine – a large bit of peppercorn would be very overpowering! Next add in the Worcestershire sauce, stir and then add the crème fraîche and stir again.

Now simply plate the dish, finishing it with a little crispy sage.

Sweet Things

Twisted tiramisu

Serves 4

My take on this classic Italian dish is like a delicious black forest gâteau – it's hard to resist!

INGREDIENTS

For the sponge fingers

4 eggs, separated

150g caster sugar

100g plain flour

½ tsp baking powder

For the tiramisu

600ml double cream

250g mascarpone

50ml Marsala wine

2 tbsp kirsch

1 tin of pitted black cherries

5 tbsp golden caster sugar

25g dark chocolate, grated

300ml espresso coffee

2 tsp cocoa powder, to garnish

Candied cherries, to garnish

METHOD

For the sponge fingers

Preheat the oven to 200°c and line a baking tray with baking paper.

Place the egg whites into a bowl and whisk until you have soft peaks. Add 2 tablespoons of sugar and continue whisking until it is shiny and you have stiff peaks.

Take another bowl and beat the egg yolks and the rest of the sugar until they are thick and pale yellow in colour. Separately, sift the flour and baking powder.

Fold half of the egg whites into the egg yolk mixture followed by the flour and baking powder. Then add the remaining egg whites and add the mixture to a piping bag. Pipe out neat evenly sized fingers onto the baking tray and bake for 7 minutes.

For the tiramisu

Whisk the cream until soft peaks form. In a separate bowl, mix the mascarpone, Marsala, kirsch, a little of the black cherry syrup and the sugar. Gently combine with the whipped cream, then stir in the chopped black cherries.

Pour the coffee into a large bowl and add half the sponge fingers. Turn them until they are soaked, but not soggy, then layer them into a large serving dish or individual bowls. Spread over half of the cream mixture and some grated chocolate.

Then soak the remaining sponge and repeat the layers, finishing with the creamy layer. Cover and chill for at least 3 hours.

To plate

Dust with cocoa and grated chocolate and decorate with candied cherries to serve.

Blackcurrant and liquorice panna cotta

Serves 4

I've livened up a simple vanilla panna cotta with a couple of Sambuca and blackcurrant infused gels plus a sprinkling of liquorice powder to tie it all together.

INGREDIENTS

For the panna cotta

3 gelatine leaves

250ml milk

250ml double cream

1 vanilla pod, split lengthways, seeds scraped out

25g sugar

For the Sambuca gel

1 gelatine leaf

100ml black Sambuca

20 crushed blackcurrants

For the garnish

A handful of blackberries, to make frozen blackberry pips

Liquorice powder

Micro fennel

METHOD

For the panna cotta

Soak the gelatine leaves in a little warm water until soft.

Next add the milk, cream, vanilla pod and sugar into a pan and heat gently. Remove the vanilla pod and set aside, next squeeze the water out of the gelatine leaves, then add them to the pan stirring until the gelatine has dissolved. Pour into moulds taking care to ensure they are all level and then place in the fridge until set, around 2 hours.

For the Sambuca gel

In a little warm water soften the gelatine leaf. Take a saucepan and bring the Sambuca to the boil and add in the crushed blackcurrants, followed by the softened gelatine, stirring until dissolved.

Pour into a flat container until it is around 1cm thick and set in the fridge, this should take around 2 hours.

For the frozen blackberries

Put some blackberries in the freezer overnight and once frozen solid burst them into little pips to garnish the dish. They don't last long so move quickly!

To plate

Sprinkle over the liquorice powder and garnish with micro fennel.

Chocolate and beetroot ice cream

Serves 4

This sounds like an unusual combination but I've found it to be a real winner. Don't forget, 24 hours before making this add your ice cream machine to the freezer if required. If you don't have this equipment, you can simply put the mixture in some tupperware in the freezer.

INGREDIENTS

For the ice cream
200g mashed fresh beetroot
100g melted dark chocolate
250ml double cream
250ml full fat milk
100g caster sugar
Pinch salt
1 vanilla pod

For the chocolate crumb
180g margarine or softened butter
180g caster sugar
3 large eggs
155g self-raising flour, sifted
50g cocoa, sifted
1 tsp baking powder

For the beetroot powder
1 packet cooked beetroot, sliced

For the garnish
Red amaranth

METHOD

For the beetroot powder
Thinly slice some cooked beetroot and place into the oven on a low heat, around 52°c, for 12 hours. When ready it should make a snap if you break one. Next add it into a processor and blitz until you have a bright pink beetroot powder to dust over your dessert.

For the ice cream
In a food processor blitz the beetroot until it is a purée to remove any excess liquid.

Next on a very low heat add some water to a saucepan and place a glass bowl over it to make a bain marie. Gently melt the chocolate and then slowly add in a little of the cream to loosen it.

In a food processor combine the milk, cream, chocolate, sugar, salt, vanilla and finally the puréed beetroot and blitz again until no bits remain. Pass this through a sieve and then add to an ice cream maker to freeze.

Wait until frozen and then let the controversy unfold...

For the chocolate crumb
Preheat the oven to 180°c.

Next, grease an 18cm round cake tin with a little butter and place a piece of greaseproof paper into the base of the tin.

Add all of the ingredients into a mixing bowl and combine with a hand-held mixer for 2 minutes. This should be enough time to make the batter smooth.

Pour the batter into the tin and bake for 45 minutes. To test it is ready, insert a skewer into the centre of the cake and it should be clean when you remove it.

Once cooled add a little cake to a food processor and blitz into a rough crumb. Keep the rest of the cake for a sweet treat at another time.

To plate
Add the chocolate crumb to the plate using a chef's ring, quenelle the ice cream on top and dust the plate with the beetroot powder.

Bananas and salted caramel hazelnut custard

Serves 4

This dish is a grown up version of everyone's childhood favourite, bananas and custard. The silky custard combined with the caramelised hazelnut crumb really brings the dish alive.

INGREDIENTS

For the custard

2 large egg yolks

2 tsp cornflour

25g caster sugar

1 vanilla pod, split lengthways

250ml whole milk

250ml double cream

For the bananas and salted caramel sauce

125g caster sugar

70g double cream

½ tsp sea salt

25g butter

Bananas

For the hazelnuts

50g sugar

30g hazelnuts

METHOD

For the custard

Add the egg yolks, cornflour and sugar to a saucepan over a medium heat. Halve the vanilla pod and then scrape the vanilla seeds into the pan, and use a metal whisk to combine all the ingredients until you have a silky paste.

Place the milk and cream in a separate pan over a low heat and cook gently for 6-8 minutes, whisking constantly. Now gradually whisk the milk and cream into the egg yolks until smooth and thick.

For the bananas and salted caramel

Add the sugar into a large frying pan and place over a medium heat until the sugar has dissolved. Turn up the heat and bubble for 2 minutes until you have caramel. Take the pan off the heat and then carefully stir in the cream, salt and butter. Slice the bananas and evenly coat them in the sauce.

For the hazelnuts

Add the sugar to a frying pan and place over a medium heat until the sugar has dissolved. Turn up the heat for 4-5 minutes until you have a golden caramel and then add the hazelnuts.

Leave on a non-stick surface to harden and then blitz in a food processor to make a caramel hazelnut crumb. You can reserve a couple of the caramelised hazelnuts whole for a garnish.

To plate

Carefully arrange the bananas around the custard with one or two whole caramelised hazelnuts and then sprinkle with the crumb.

Maple dulce de leche with caramelised pears and pistachio popcorn

Serves 4

This is one for those with a real sweet tooth, combining the syrupy dulce de leche with caramelised pears and light fluffy popcorn. The addition of a milk skin crisp will make this a stand out dinner party dish.

INGREDIENTS

For the maple dulce de leche
1 can sweetened condensed milk

1 tbsp maple syrup

For the pears
75g caster sugar

25g butter

2 firm pears, peeled

For the caramel sauce
125g caster sugar

70ml double cream

25g butter

For the pistachio popcorn
1 tbsp sunflower oil

50g popping corn

50g pistachios, blitzed in a food processor

For the milk skin crisps
300ml whole milk

Baking paper, lightly rubbed with vegetable oil

METHOD

For the maple dulce de leche
Preheat the oven to 220°c. Pour the condensed milk and maple syrup into a 20cm round pie dish and cover with foil. Put the dish into a roasting tray half full with water and bake for one hour. You will know it's ready when the milk is golden in colour.

For the caramelised pears
In a large frying pan add the sugar and heat until softened and golden. Add the butter and pears then fry, stirring regularly until tender and covered in a sticky glaze.

For the caramel sauce
Tip the sugar into a frying pan and place over a medium heat until the sugar has dissolved into a caramel and it is golden in colour. Remove from the heat and carefully stir in the cream and butter. Leave the sauce to cool a little and then add into a squeezy bottle.

For the pistachio popcorn
Use a heavy-based pot with a sturdy handle and a tight glass fitting lid. Put the pot over a medium heat. Add the oil and corn. Put the lid on and heat, shaking occasionally, until it starts to pop. Remove from heat when all of the corn has popped, being careful not to burn the kernels. Drizzle with the caramel sauce and sprinkle with the pistachio dust.

For the milk skin crisps
Over a medium heat, bring the milk to boil, then sieve into a large frying pan and place over a low heat until the milk begins to form a skin. This should take about 8 minutes.

Use a knife to break the skin away from the pan. Now take the baking paper and place on top of the milk skin, it will stick to the paper.

Lift the paper off the milk and place with the skin facing upwards onto a baking tray. Place into the oven on the lowest possible setting with the door open to dry out, this should take about an hour.

To plate
First add the sauce to the plate, then the pears with the popcorn on top. Finally gently rest the milk skin crisp on an angle.

Ma hor pineapple with coconut

Serves 4

Ma hor translates as 'galloping horses' and is a popular Thai appetiser supposedly named after King Rama VII's excellent horsemanship. I've adapted it for a dessert by substituting the pork for caramelised nuts and adding some meringue, coconut and coriander sugar.

INGREDIENTS

For the Italian meringue
4 egg whites
225g caster sugar
100ml water

For the cashew nut brittle
100g cashew nuts
100g caster sugar

For the pineapple
100g caster sugar
80g golden syrup
1 red chilli, sliced julienne
80ml pineapple juice
1 pineapple, cut into rectangles

For the coconut cream
1 tin/carton coconut cream

For the coriander sugar
Small bunch micro coriander, retain some for garnish
50g sugar

METHOD

For the Italian meringue
Whisk the egg whites in a bowl with an electric mixer until firm peaks form.

Next place the sugar and water into a saucepan and slowly bring to the boil until the syrup reaches 120°c on a sugar thermometer, then remove the pan from the heat. Now extremely carefully, while whisking the egg whites, pour in the sugar syrup in a steady stream and continue whisking for 2 minutes until the meringue has cooled slightly.

You can add this to the plate and give it a nice glaze with a blow torch if you have one.

For the cashew nut brittle
Pour the sugar into a saucepan and place it onto a low heat. Shake the pan a little as it starts to melt but do not stir it or be tempted to add water. Be patient, make sure you are watching it at all times. It will slowly start to turn caramel in colour once all the sugar is dissolved, resulting in a sticky sauce. Add the cashew nuts and pour out onto a thin non-stick surface.

You can either serve this in chunks or process it into a rough crumb to sprinkle over the finished dish.

For the pineapple
In a saucepan over a medium heat, combine the sugar, golden syrup, chilli (reserve some for garnish) and pineapple juice. Heat until simmering and then add in the pineapple, and glaze for 3 minutes.

For the coconut cream
Separate the thick cream and add it to a small piping bag.

For the coriander sugar
Add a small bunch of coriander to a food processor with the sugar and blitz until the coriander is broken down and the sugar is green in colour.

To plate
Top the neatly sliced pineapple with the cashew nuts and add a chilli slice to each side. Garnish with micro coriander, arrange the meringue and sugar around it then finally pipe the coconut cream alongside.

Mint chocolate soufflé

Serves 4

This rich indulgent French dessert always goes down well at the end of a meal.

INGREDIENTS

For the crème pâtissière

Unsalted butter, for the ramekins

25g good quality dark chocolate

2 tbsp plain flour

2 tsp caster sugar

½ tsp cornflour

1 medium egg yolk

1 medium whole egg

For the ganache

50g good quality dark chocolate, preferably 70% cocoa solids, broken into pieces

4 tbsp milk

4 tbsp double cream

1 tbsp of cocoa

1 tbsp fresh mint, finely chopped

For the egg whites

6 medium egg whites

85g caster sugar

METHOD

Firstly, chill your ramekins for 30 minutes. This will help the butter adhere to them quickly and prevent sticking. In a saucepan melt a little unsalted butter and then remove your ramekins from the fridge. Brush them with softened butter in an upward motion.

Chill the dishes for 5 more minutes and repeat this step. Then grate a little chocolate into each dish, so that it sticks to the butter. Rotate the dish around, tilting it as you do so the ramekin it is evenly coated.

For the crème pâtissière

Mix together the flour, sugar and cornflour. Then put the egg yolk and the whole egg into a bowl and combine. Add in half of the flour mixture to create a smooth paste, then add in the rest of the flour mixture and whisk until smooth.

For the ganache

Chop the chocolate into small pieces. In a saucepan add the milk and cream and bring just to the boil. Remove from the heat and add the chopped chocolate. Leave for a minute and it will melt quite quickly. Stir continuously and slowly add in the cocoa. Set aside, allow the mixture to cool and then add in the very finely chopped mint.

Heat oven to 190°c. In a completely clean bowl whisk the egg whites to soft peaks. As you're mixing, sprinkle in the sugar. Once the sugar is combined, keep whisking to give stiff, firm peaks. At this point if you are brave enough, check you have done it right by holding the bowl over your head – the mixture shouldn't fall out.

Mix the crème pâtissière and ganache together in a large bowl and then vigorously stir in 2 tablespoons of egg white. Very gently fold in a third of the rest, cutting through the mixture. Fold in another third very gently so you don't knock the air out of it, and then fold in the rest.

Add the mixture into the ramekins. Fill them a quarter of the way from the top, and then bang each dish gently on your work surface. Then top up the mixture and tap gently again. Use your thumb to run a small indentation around the top of the mixture just to move it away from the rim of the bowl. Bake the soufflés for 15-17 minutes.

When they are done, dust with icing sugar and serve immediately.

Peanut parfait with a trio of cherry

Serves 4

This dish has a lot of different steps but if you take your time you will end up with a melt in the mouth parfait, made all the more delicious by my sumptuously sweet cherry additions.

INGREDIENTS

For the peanut parfait

120ml whole milk

4 large eggs, separated

75g granulated sugar

250ml whipping cream

150g smooth peanut butter

25g unsalted peanuts, chopped

For the cherry dust

1 packet freeze dried red cherries

For the candied cherries

200g black cherries

100g caster sugar

80g golden syrup

80ml cherry juice

For the cherry coulis

100g cherries, chopped

84ml cherry juice

85g caster sugar

½ lemon, juiced

2g xanthan gum (available from Amazon)

METHOD

For the parfait

Pour the milk into a saucepan and heat gently. Meanwhile, whisk the egg yolks with the sugar in a large bowl, until pale and creamy. When the milk comes to the boil, pour it onto the egg yolks, whisking all the time. Pour the mixture into a clean pan and stir over a low heat until it has thickened enough to coat the back of a spoon. Be careful not to overheat the mixture. Allow to cool.

In a bowl, whip the cream to soft peaks. In a separate bowl, whip the egg whites until they form soft peaks. Mix the peanut butter into the egg yolk mixture, then gently fold in the whipped cream followed by the egg whites. When thoroughly combined, transfer the parfait to a suitable container, cover and freeze for at least 6 hours.

For the cherry dust

Simply add the freeze dried cherries into a food processor and blitz until you have a powder.

For the candied cherries

In a saucepan, over medium to high heat, combine the sugar, golden syrup and cherry juice. Heat until boiling and let it reduce by half until thick and sticky. Now carefully using the stalk of the cherries, dip them into the glaze a couple of times so that they are nice and shiny.

You can retain this syrup to garnish your dish.

For the cherry coulis

Add all of the cherry coulis ingredients to a pan and bring to the boil. Allow to cool slightly and then carefully pass through a sieve and add to a squeezy bottle ready to plate up your dish.

To plate

Dust the plate with cherry dust, add the parfait and two dots of coulis placing the candied cherry on one of them.

The art of plating

You begin to taste with your eyes before a morsel of food even hits your taste buds, so it's really important to take as much care plating up as you do preparing and cooking your meal. Here are a few tips of mine to ensure your dish looks as good as it tastes.

List of useful equipment
- Circular and square cutters
- Tweezers
- Blow torch
- Piping bag
- Pipette
- Peeler/spiraliser
- Squeezy bottle
- Chef's ring

The first thing you need to do is organise all of the elements and ingredients of your dish, and make sure you have a bowl for things like off-cuts. This is called mise en place, which translates to everything in its place. If you're organised, then you'll be less likely to rush and make mistakes.

Sharpen your knives; this will give you a cleaner cut.

Make sure your plate or dish is as clean as possible. Keep a clean towel or kitchen paper handy for wiping up any spillages, drips or oil.

Practice first. If you're piping, drizzling or swiping sauce across the plate, it might take one or two attempts before it looks as professional as you're aiming for.

When using a squeezy bottle to sauce a dish do not move it around, just pull it straight up. Raising vertically like this will avoid an unattractive swirl. When swiping sauce, a warm spoon often helps with making it neat.

Take time and care positioning. I like to keep the size and shape of individual elements uniform, and symmetry looks great where possible.

Be picky; if an ingredient or garnish doesn't look right use another piece. It's little details that keep things neat.

When using herbs, especially micro herbs, make sure they are as fresh as possible, and not discoloured or wilted. Take time to find the best leaves and use tweezers to apply them to the dish.

If you're worried there's not enough on the plate, or that you have a lot leftover after plating so precisely, simply put the extras into serving dishes for the middle of the table. This will satisfy the hungrier guest whilst still maintaining a stunning plate of food.

Finally, these are just guidelines, there are no strict rules. Don't be scared to change your mind as to how you want it to look as you go along, as this is your chance to be creative. Have a go at whatever comes to mind and play with texture, size, placement and balance. The aim is to show off each element of the dish, and make it look appealing to you personally – you'll be the one eating it after all!

See for yourself

Have a look at the following dishes. They're actually very simple to make, but have been plated up to look extraordinary.

1. Curry spiced new potato and turmeric egg salad, page 22.

This dish grew from a love of a simple potato salad, or a classic egg and chips combination. It shows how being selective over ingredients like the purple potatoes and careful with positioning makes all the difference.

2. Simply curried cauliflower, page 136.

This one is all about texture and layers. It looks visually stunning, even though it has been made using predominately just one ingredient.

3. Gyros pork with flat breads and oregano tzatziki, page 116.

This is a good example of plating in a trio formation to make it as uniform and symmetrical as possible. I've also gone to that extra effort of cutting the flatbreads into triangles.

4. Crispy lamb salad with baba ganoush and flatbread, page 24.

This is essentially a lamb kebab that's been plated up to look as elegant as it tastes.

1.

2.

3.

4.

The Next Level

Baba ganoush

Rich, smoky and creamy, this Middle-Eastern dish is a great addition to lamb.

INGREDIENTS

1 whole bulb garlic

3 large aubergines

½ lemon, juiced

3 tbsp tahini paste

1 pinch ground cumin

3 tbsp extra virgin olive oil

Sea salt, to taste

White pepper

1 pinch smoked paprika

1 tbsp fresh flat-leaf parsley, chopped

METHOD

Preheat your oven to 170°c and slow roast the garlic until softened.

Prick the aubergines with a fork and place under a hot grill until the skin is charred and blackened. Then place in the oven at 170°c for 15 minutes, or until the flesh feels soft when you press it.

In a pestle and mortar, crush 3 cloves of the sweet roasted garlic with the lemon juice, tahini, cumin, olive oil and salt and pepper.

When cool enough to handle, cut the aubergines in half and scoop out the flesh.

Add the softened part of the warm aubergines into the pestle and mortar with the remaining ingredients.

Place in a serving dish and finish with a drizzle of olive oil and sprinkle the paprika and parsley over the top, before finishing with a drizzle of olive oil.

Balsamic bacon bits

We all need a little something that is just that extra bit special every now and then, something that makes our dishes sparkle, these mini balsamic pancetta lardons are just that.

INGREDIENTS

All you need is two ingredients;

A really good thick sticky and sweet balsamic vinegar, I use Belazu

Some good quality pancetta lardons

METHOD

In a dry saucepan add the pancetta, you don't need to add any oil as there's plenty within the meat. Stirring gently brown these off until the fat is foaming and bubbly. This is when you need to move quickly. Drain off just over half of the fat, return to the heat and add in two tablespoons of the balsamic vinegar. It should evenly coat each lardon so it looks shiny. Cook for a few more seconds and then pour out onto a baking tray to cool. Store in the fridge and add to any salad or pasta dish to give it that extra layer of texture and flavour.

Burnt leeks and caramelised shallots

Both of these can be used to add height and texture to a dish; the bitter sweetness will provide an amazing flavour hit to your dishes.

INGREDIENTS

Leeks
Shallots

METHOD

For the leeks

For the leeks, heat your oven to 200°c. Remove the root of the leek and slice a 12cm piece out of the white section. Next halve this and lay the first three layers of the leek flat. At 5mm intervals slice lengthways to give you a perfect stick. Lay your leeks out on a baking sheet lined with parchment and bake in the oven until crispy and dark brown.

For the shallots

Caramelised shallots look amazing and also go really well with the crispy sage leaves. Firstly halve your shallot from top to bottom; don't remove the papery skin, it will help them steam inside. Next lay a piece of foil into a large frying pan and on a high heat place the shallots the cut-side down. There's no need to use any oil. I like to weigh mine down with a heavy saucepan to ensure good even contact. In about 5 minutes check them and you will see the cut-side is now blackened and the inside has steamed and become soft. Peel off the skin and separate each layer to serve as an eye catching accompaniment.

Caramelised chicory

These are really simple and add a great dimension to any dish. There are just a couple of steps to making sure you get perfectly caramelised chicories every time, here's how I make them.

INGREDIENTS

2 white chicories
Caster sugar
Olive oil
25g butter

METHOD

For the chicory, remove any damaged outer leaves and cut in half lengthways.
Heat a small amount of olive oil in a hot frying pan. Sprinkle a little caster sugar over the cut surface of the chicories and place in the hot frying pan, cut-side down. Cover with greaseproof paper and when the surface is golden add in a knob of butter and baste over the top of the chicory until evenly coated and softened.

Chorizo crumb

As far as next level additions go, this one has to be by far the easiest to make, and it so happens to be my personal favourite. A chorizo crumb brings a powerful punch of flavour to many different dishes; you also end up with a nice oil to use as a dressing to accompany the dish.

INGREDIENTS

Chorizo
Olive Oil

METHOD

This is so simple to make that you can afford to spend a little time on the prep. I prefer the chorizo to be diced uniformly into chunks of around 5mm square – the devil is in the detail and little accurate touches like this will give the dish that wow factor!

Once you have diced your chorizo simply add a tablespoon of olive oil into a large cold frying pan followed by your chorizo. I use a cold pan as this allows the oil in the chorizo to warm through gently and render down into that lovely dressing for your dish.

Once the chorizo is brown and crispy, drain onto some kitchen paper and store the oil in a jar to use later.

Crispy onions

These are really simple to make and add that extra dimension to any dish. I like to use shallots but this works equally well with any kind of onion.

INGREDIENTS

Onions
Salt
Cornflour

METHOD

Finely chop or slice the onion and add them to a large mixing bowl. Season really heavily with salt and leave for 3-4 hours.

At this point you will see the moisture come out of the onions. Simply wash off all of the salt and lay out to partially dry on a cloth or piece of kitchen paper.

Dust the onion gently in cornflour and set aside on some greaseproof paper.

Now here is my secret: if you drop these straight into a deep pan of hot oil they will burn before the onion is cooked. What I do is drop them into cold oil and heat them up gradually; by the time the oil is up to temperature they are crispy, golden and delicious. Simply drain on to kitchen paper and serve.

Herb crisps

Crispy leafy herbs make wonderful additions to most dishes, however you must be careful as some leaves like basil contain a lot of water and can spit during cooking. My personal favourite is sage as it works wonderfully well with pork.

INGREDIENTS

Leafy herbs of your choice.

METHOD

Take some time selecting the leaves you will be using. If you are cooking for four or six people make sure they are all the same size. It is little things like this that will take your home cooking to the next level. Have some kitchen paper ready and carefully but simply drop the leaves into some hot oil. Remove after around 20-30 seconds and drain immediately.

Holy guacamole

Perfect as a dip for nachos or as an accompaniment to other spicy dishes.

INGREDIENTS

1 red chilli, de-seeded and finely chopped

2 tbsp fresh coriander, finely chopped

2 limes, juice and zest

2 ripe, soft avocados

1 tsp smoked paprika

Sea salt and white pepper

METHOD

Finely chop the chilli and coriander, making sure you wash your hands afterwards. Zest the limes, taking care to only get the green skin and not the white pith. Set aside with the chilli and coriander.

On your kitchen work surface roll the limes under the palm of your hand to break down the inside, enabling you to get more juice out of them. Now juice the limes and set the liquid aside. Don't worry if it looks like a lot, you want a really zingy guacamole.

Halve your avocado lengthways. When you hit the large stone in the middle, twist the avocado in two and carefully chop into the stone with your knife and twist sideways to remove it. Scoop out the flesh.

Now all you have to do is simply combine all of the ingredients into a smooth paste, either in a food processor or with a potato masher or a fork.

Panna gratta

Panna gratta is a great way of using up leftover bread and adding extra texture to any pasta dish or salad.

INGREDIENTS

Stale ciabatta
Olive oil
Garlic clove
Sea salt

METHOD

Take a stale ciabatta and either chop or use a processor to break down into small bite size pieces and crumbs.

In a large frying pan add 3 tablespoons of oil and heat gently. With your knife crush a garlic clove just enough to crack it open and fry off until just brown. At that point remove it from the oil and add in the breadcrumbs. Coat evenly and season with sea salt. Once they are starting to brown put them on a baking tray and toast gently in the oven for 10 minutes at 150°c until dry and crunchy. These will keep for months in an airtight container.

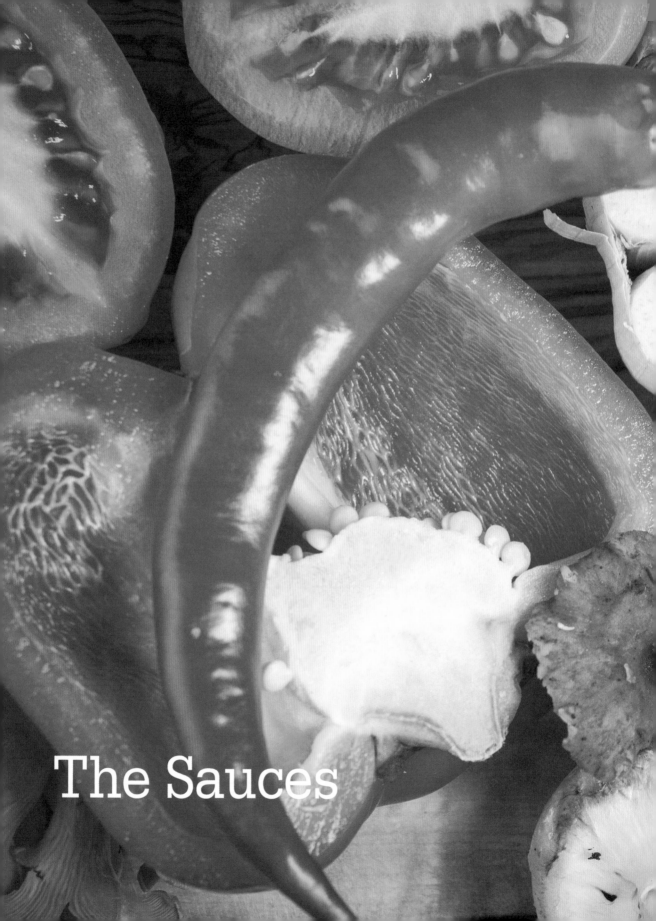

The Sauces

Arrabiata

A classic Italian sauce combining ripe tomatoes with fresh herbs and fiery chilli. Great to keep in for quick mid-week pasta dinners.

INGREDIENTS

1 tbsp, olive oil

2 cloves garlic, crushed into a paste

2 shallots, finely diced

1 tsp fresh thyme

2 tsp fresh oregano

2 red chillies, finely chopped

1 tbsp tomato purée

2 ½ tsp smoked paprika

10 ripe cherry tomatoes, quartered

1 litre passata

1 tin chopped tomatoes

70g fresh basil, chopped

Sea salt and white pepper

METHOD

In a large saucepan gently heat the olive oil then add in the garlic paste. Stir gently for around 20 seconds, then add the shallots and soften gently for a couple of minutes.

Once the shallots are softened, add in the thyme, oregano and chillies. Cook this out for another minute, then add in the tomato purée and smoked paprika.

Cook for another minute, stirring frequently.

Next add the quartered cherry tomatoes, passata and tin of chopped tomatoes. Cook the sauce gently for 15 minutes then stir in the chopped basil and cook for another 20 seconds, then season and serve.

Béchamel

A basic white sauce is one of the first things every chef learns, and can be used as a base for other sauces.

INGREDIENTS

600ml milk

1 bay leaf (optional)

1 pinch fresh nutmeg, grated

60g butter

60g plain flour

Salt and freshly ground black pepper, to taste

METHOD

Firstly, in a saucepan heat the milk with the bay leaf and nutmeg, taking care that it doesn't boil over.

Next melt the butter in a large saucepan over a low heat. Once melted gently sift in the flour stirring all the time until you have a thick paste. Cook the paste out, moving continuously for a couple of minutes.

Using a ladle slowly whisk in a little of the infused milk at a time, stirring continuously until you have a smooth, slightly thick sauce. Remove from the heat, remove the bay leaf and season with salt and pepper.

Carbonara

You have to be quick and precise with this sauce to avoid scrambling the eggs. Once you've perfected it though I guarantee it will become a firm favourite in your dinner party repertoire.

INGREDIENTS

100g diced pancetta

3 medium eggs

5 tbsp single cream

3 tbsp ricotta cheese

4 tbsp finely grated Parmesan cheese

Sea salt and freshly ground white pepper

METHOD

Firstly, in a dry frying pan gently fry the pancetta until it has browned and the fat cooks out, and then drain on some kitchen paper.

In a bowl mix together the eggs, single cream, ricotta and half of the Parmesan and season just a little – take care with the salt as the pancetta will add salt to the dish anyway.

To finish this sauce, you need to wait until you have drained your pasta, retaining a little of the cooking water. Then gently stir in the cream and egg mixture. You need to do this off the heat otherwise you'll get scrambled eggs.

Finally stir in the pancetta, sprinkle with the remaining Parmesan and add a twist of white pepper to serve.

Classic tomato

Stir into pasta, use as a pizza base or transform it into a delicious soup.

INGREDIENTS

1 tbsp olive oil

2 cloves garlic, crushed into a paste

2 shallots, finely diced

3 tsp fresh oregano

1 tbsp tomato purée

10 ripe cherry tomatoes, quartered

1 litre passata

1 tin chopped tomatoes

70g fresh basil, chopped

Sea salt and white pepper

METHOD

In a large saucepan gently heat the olive oil and then add in the garlic paste. Stir gently for around 20 seconds, then add in the shallots and soften gently for a couple of minutes.

Once the shallots are softened add in the oregano and tomato purée and cook for another minute stirring frequently. Next add the quartered cherry tomatoes, the passata and the tin of chopped tomatoes. Cook the sauce gently for 15 minutes, stir in the chopped basil and cook for another 20 seconds. Season and then serve.

Creamy mushroom

Earthy, rich and buttery, this sauce is great with pasta, chicken or steak.

INGREDIENTS

1 tbsp olive oil

15g butter

2 cloves garlic, peeled and crushed into a paste

2 shallots, peeled and finely chopped

225g chestnut mushrooms, brushed and sliced

½ tsp fresh sage

1 tbsp fresh thyme

150ml dry vermouth

150ml crème fraîche

1 tbsp freshly chopped parsley

Sea salt and white pepper

METHOD

Gently heat the oil and butter in a large frying pan. Add in the garlic paste and stir gently for around 20 seconds. Next add in the shallots and soften gently for a couple of minutes.

Add the mushrooms, sage and thyme and cook for 5 minutes until the mushrooms just start to soften. Next add in the vermouth and reduce by half. Finally stir in your crème fraîche and parsley until warm, then season to taste with sea salt and ground white pepper.

Pesto

You can't beat fresh pesto, so I make sure I always have a batch in to add as a garnish to meat dishes, salads or stirred into pasta.

INGREDIENTS

50g pine nuts

2 cloves garlic

Pinch sea salt

Two large bunches basil

50g Parmesan

150ml olive oil

½ lemon, juiced

METHOD

In a large frying pan toast the pine nuts until golden.

Next use the back of your knife to crush the garlic into a smooth paste. A little sea salt will help to do this.

I make my pesto in a food processor, but you can use a pestle and mortar. With the exception of the lemon juice add in all the remaining ingredients and blitz into a smooth paste. Taste and add the lemon juice and adjust the seasoning accordingly.

This will go amazingly well with pasta, meat or roasted vegetables.

Roasted red pepper

A sweeter alternative to a tomato sauce.

INGREDIENTS

8 red peppers

1 tbsp olive oil

2 cloves garlic, crushed into a paste

2 shallots, finely diced

2 tsp fresh oregano

1 tbsp tomato purée

1 tsp smoked paprika

1 litre passata

70g fresh basil, chopped

Sea salt and white pepper

METHOD

Either under a grill or over a gas flame using some tongues blacken the skin on the red peppers. Once they are black, place immediately in a food bag and seal for a few minutes to steam.

Remove them from the bag and scrape off the black skin and remove any seeds. This is a little bit of work but it is worth the extra effort.

Add the peeled roasted peppers to a food processor and blitz into a paste, or if you have time chop through with a large knife until you have the same consistency.

Now, in a large saucepan gently heat the olive oil and then add in the garlic paste. Stir gently for around 20 seconds, then add in the shallots and soften gently for a couple of minutes.

Once the shallots are softened add in the oregano and stir for another minute. Then add in the tomato purée and smoked paprika, stirring frequently. Add the red peppers and passata and cook the sauce gently for 15 minutes. Stir in the chopped basil and cook for another 20 seconds. Season and then serve.

Index